"Not since Hemingway have I read a more exciting journal of great food, drink, friends, and life. The storytelling made me feel as if I were there with her, and, now, I wish I had been."
—Donald Link, author of *Real Cajun* and chef owner of New Orleans' acclaimed Herbsaint and Cochon restaurants

"If this doesn't make you hungry and thirsty, call the doctor, you are sick." —Roy Blount Jr.

ALSO BY JULIA REED

Ham Biscuits, Hostess Gowns, and Other Southern Specialties: An Entertaining Life (with Recipes)

The House on First Street: My New Orleans Story

Queen of the Turtle Derby and Other Southern Phenomena

Praise for *But Mama Always Put Vodka in Her Sangria!*

"Reed's reflections and anecdotes are siren calls to the kitchen, an experience heightened by her delight in sharing tales of a Southern upbringing." —*Publishers Weekly* (starred review)

"Julia Reed could make boiled newspaper sound delicious. . . . She gives each meal a juicy backstory and characters you wish you'd stayed up all night carousing with, making it the stuff of legend and not just a midnight snack. Her latest essay collection is a sensory delight and fantasia for aspiring chefs, but it's also bighearted and fun." —*BookPage*

"Julia Reed is a unique figure in American life and letters. No one writes better about the art of hospitality and the centrality of food, drink, and good company—the things that make our hours glow and our souls sound. With wit, insight, and a sure sense of the human condition, Julia is an indispensable guide to living well."

—Jon Meacham, Pulitizer Prize–winning author of *Thomas Jefferson: The Art of Power*

"Julia Reed is on the loose again, this time discoursing as savvily and fearlessly and hilariously as always on the unquestionable superiority of Southern cookery, the social status of the gin martini, Spanish paprika, and a few dozen other matters of some urgency. With each collection of essays, 'Miss Julia' just gets better and better, a voice that never loses its originality, freshness, and supreme wit."

—James Villas, author of *Pig: King of the Southern Table*

BUT MAMA ALWAYS

PUT VODKA

in Her

SANGRIA!

• • •

Adventures in *Eating,*
Drinking, and
Making Merry

• • •

Julia Reed

St. Martin's Griffin ⚞ New York

www.stmartins.com

Designed by Nicola Ferguson

The Library of Congress has cataloged the hardcover edition as follows:

Reed, Julia.

But Mama always put vodka in her sangria! : adventures in eating, drinking, and making merry / Julia Reed.

   p. cm.

Includes index.

ISBN 978-1-250-01904-2 (hardcover)

ISBN 978-1-250-01905-9 (e-book)

1. Gastronomy. 2. Food—Social aspects. 3. Food habits. 4. Drinking customs. 5. Dinners and dining. 6. Cooking. 7. Alcoholic beverages. 8. Reed, Julia—Travel. I. Title.

TX631.R33 2013

641.2'1—dc23

2013009266

ISBN 978-1-250-04903-2 (trade paperback)

St. Martin's Griffin books may be purchased for educational, business, or promotional use. For information on bulk purchases, please contact Macmillan Corporate and Premium Sales Department at 1-800-221-7945, extension 5442, or write specialmarkets@macmillan.com.

First St. Martin's Griffin Edition: June 2014

D 10 9 8 7 6 5 4

For my parents,
Judy and Clarke Reed

*And in joyful memory of
Anne Ross and Burrell McGee*

Contents

. . . And Making Merry

Acknowledgments

This book's title comes from a story involving Elizabeth McGee Cordes and her mother, Anne Ross McGee. I've spent my entire life celebrating birthdays and Christmases and countless other occasions with Elizabeth and her sister Anne. We grew up in each other's houses and when I first began spending time in New Orleans more than twenty years ago, I spent more restorative hours at Elizabeth's kitchen table than in any local restaurant. I am endlessly grateful for my relationship with Elizabeth and Anne and Elizabeth's daughters Katie and Lizzy, as well as with the entire extended McGee clan. They have all enriched my life immeasurably.

The list of cooks and food writers, hosts and hostesses to whom I owe a great debt is far too long to mention here, but I must single out a few. Lottie Martin, Ernestine Turner, and Martha Wilhoite nurtured me in spirit and in body and taught me everything I know about the connection between cooking and caring and love. For his friendship and generosity and unparalleled way around a stove, I thank Donald Link. The life-enhancing staff at each of his restaurants also contributes mightily to my well-being.

Jon Meacham asked me to write the column in *Newsweek* where many of these essays were born and provides invaluable counsel on almost every matter—except for food and drink. He leaves those subjects to his wife, Keith, and me, whom he has dubbed (not without a tiny bit of derision) the "Crabmeat Caucus." Keith is an uncommonly loyal friend, staunch running buddy, and tireless cohostess, and I can't imagine anyone with whom I'd rather caucus.

Thanks to Elizabeth Nichols, Mary Catherine McClellan, and Mark McDonald, who asked me to be a part of Taigan .com, where some of these essays and recipes appeared in slightly different form on *Fetch*. I am also grateful to the great Joni Evans and my colleagues on wowowow.com, where I tried out more of what you see on these pages.

For kindnesses large and small, as well as many memorable meals and shindigs, thanks to Mary Thomas Joseph, Robert Harling, Howard Brent, Eden Brent, Taylor Haxton, Suzanne and Fred Rheinstein, Byron and Cameron Seward, Amanda and Carl Cottingham, Robert Jenkins, Mary Sferruzza, Richard and Lisa Howorth, Jason Epstein, Liz Smith, Joe Armstrong, Ben and Libby Page, Jeremiah Tower, James Villas, Annette Tapert and Joe Allen, Peter Patout, Peter Rogers, Joyce and Rod Wilson, Joe and Candy Ledbetter, Debra and Jerry Shriver, Ti Martin, Lally Brennan, Juan Luis and Jenny Hernandez, John Alexander, Bill Dunlap and Linda Burgess, Maggie Dunlap, Jay McInerney, Amanda Hesser, John Harris, Beth Biundo, Cathy and Gary Smith, Charles Modica, Florence Signa, Patrick Dunne, and Ken Smith.

This is my second book for Michael Flamini at St. Martin's, whom I first met when he asked me to write the foreword to *The New York Times Chicken Cookbook*. From that first conversation I realized we were food-obsessed kindred spirits. Not only has he been my great champion, he has been a great friend and intrepid dining companion. I want to thank Amanda Urban for her friendship, her invariably wise counsel, and her seemingly bottomless patience with me. Thanks as well to the inimitable and joyous Bebe Howorth, who served as my assistant and so much more.

Jessica Brent has not only served as cohostess of some wildly memorable parties with me and for me, she has been the best lifelong copilot anyone could hope for. My husband, John Pearce, supported me in this endeavor and so very much more and will forever be my favorite cohost. This book is dedicated to my parents, Judy and Clarke Reed, whose humor, warmth, and generosity of spirit (and otherwise) are impossible to exaggerate. I am so grateful that the party on Bayou Road is still going.

Introduction

Several years ago, I came back from a trip to Spain with a suitcase full of contraband *jamón ibérico* and a head full of at least half a dozen recipes I wanted to try. When I called to invite my friend Elizabeth McGee Cordes to the Spanish dinner party I'd decided to throw, she immediately volunteered to make the sangria. Now, I have never been a big sangria drinker or maker, so when she arrived on the designated evening with two pitchers in hand, I put them on the bar in the courtyard of the French Quarter house where I was then living, brought out a few plates of hors d'oeuvres, and went back in the kitchen to finish cooking. I swear I wasn't inside for more than twenty minutes, but when I emerged I found most of the guests in varying degrees of disarray—talking way too loudly, touching each other far too affectionately, carrying on in ways not usually brought on by a glass or two of red wine punch. "What in the world did you put in the sangria?" I asked a still-standing Elizabeth. "Vodka," she replied brightly, as though it were a perfectly normal—indeed, standard—addition. I knew people added a bit of Grand Marnier or Triple Sec to sangria, and sometimes brandy, too, but I had never heard of anyone pouring in an entire fifth of vodka as turned out to be the case in this instance. My jaw dropped. "Vodka??" Yes, she said, as though it were a ridiculous question. "Mama always put vodka in her sangria."

The mama in this story is Anne Ross Gee McGee, otherwise known as "Bossy," and who, alas, is no longer with us. In addition to being the mother of Elizabeth and her sister, Anne—to whom I refer in life and on these pages as "McGee"—Anne Ross was my mother's closest friend and my own chief protector and confidant, taking a far more circumspect view of my adolescent shenanigans than either of my parents. Bossy had been well schooled in all points of social etiquette by her mother, "Little Anne," but she herself was larger than life— a smart, seductive, and funny, funny woman, three parts Mame and one part Maggie the Cat. So it was that when Elizabeth explained about the vodka, I fell over laughing and told her it ought to be the title of her autobiography.

Instead, it's the title of this book, indicative of both our mothers' extraordinarily generous approaches not just to entertaining but to life its own self and a tribute to the expansive way in which we were lucky enough to have been brought up. And while it's a funny line, there are countless more just like it: But Mama said it was fine to turn the attic into a grocery store; Mama said it was okay to stage *The Tonight Show* in the living room; of course Mama said we could sell beer at our lemonade stand (to be fair, they didn't know what exactly we were selling until after the fact). They took us with them to movies like *Reflections in a Golden Eye* that we were far too young to see, and never once picked us up from school on time because they were always, um, busy. When Steve McQueen was filming *The Reivers* in Anne Ross's hometown of Carroll-ton, Mississippi, they drove over, determined to meet him. Af-ter bribing a guard with a case of beer, they crept onto the set—a cattle pasture—"disguised" by the tree branches they held in front of them. When the unsettled cows began moo-ing, shooting was stopped and the scene ruined, but McQueen was so amused by these clearly crazy but good-looking women, he invited them to eat lunch with him in the commissary.

No matter what else they were up to, they found time to give us birthday parties with ponies and piñatas, and calypso parties with the outfits and instruments they brought us back from Jamaica. They gave us Easter dinner parties featuring votive candles they'd made by filling blown-out eggs with lay-ers of pastel-colored wax; they made us homemade chefs' hats for our cookouts. For themselves, they threw the first twist party in town, created a Mexican wedding reception for Anne Ross's niece, and put on so many rehearsal dinners for the chil-dren of their friends they should have hung out a shingle. Anne Ross was a big proponent of back-to-back events—the house was already clean, she reasoned, and the flowers not dead yet—but mostly she and my mother took turns. Anne Ross and her husband, the beloved Burrell (aka "Teeny Bubba"—yes, we have a lot of nicknames), were in charge of the Christmas Eve party; my parents held the bash on Christmas night.

At both holiday events we were not only dressed up and in attendance, we were given sparkling Catawba juice in champagne flutes until we were old enough to imbibe the real thing with the grown-ups. When I was sixteen, I helped Anne Ross throw my father's fiftieth birthday party; nine years later we cohosted my mother's surprise bash complete with a Queen for a Day theme and a rattan "throne" bedecked with flowers. It was that intergenerational nature of almost every gathering that made them so special—and so edifying to us—and it's a tradition Elizabeth and I try to maintain to this day. At my father's enormous sixtieth birthday shindig, for example, part of the entertainment was a performance by the Satin Dolls, a girl group comprised of my friends and me who performed a rewritten version of our namesake song ("Silver-haired cool cat, he slays me . . ."); at his more intimate eightieth, held at the '21' Club twenty years later, Elizabeth's daughter Katie filled in for a missing Doll. The latter event became the subject of a *Wall Street Journal* column by Peggy Noonan lamenting "the end of placeness," in which she cited our birthday group as the exception. "Most of the people there were from the South, different ages and generations but Southerners—the men grounded and courteous in a certain way, the women sleeveless and sexy in a certain way," she wrote. "There was a lot of singing and toasting and drinking, and this was the thing: Even as an outsider, you knew them. They were Mississippi Delta people—Mizz-izz-DEHLT people—and the sense of placeness they brought into the room with them was sweet to me."

It was sweet of Peggy to pen such a tribute to our raucous crowd, but the truth is that I've long known how blessed I am to have come from such a place, a place populated with extraordinary people like my parents and the McGee clan and filled with all the action they were forever getting up to. It was a place that gave me all the stuff I needed for venturing out into the wider world, and when I got there I was lucky enough to gain even more mentors in both the kitchen and the dining room, ranging from Susan Mary Alsop to Jason Epstein, who is the subject of one of these essays.

Still, no one could have matched my original mentors Anne Ross and my mother, Judy, from whom Elizabeth and McGee and I learned the fine art of entertaining not just other folks but ourselves as well. Putting vodka in the sangria is as good a place as any to start, I suppose, and, as it turns out, it's not so crazy as it sounds. In his excellent drinks book *Mix Shake Stir,* Danny Meyer adds both rum and gin to his version. Below, I add rum to Anne Ross's version and slack off just a tad on the vodka. It's good enough to have made a sangria convert out of me and every time I drink it I make a silent toast to the much-missed Bossy.

MCGEE MEMORIAL SANGRIA

(*Yield: About 3 quarts*)

2 bottles Rioja, or any other full-bodied, dry red wine

1 cup simple syrup

1 cup brandy

½ cup Grand Marnier

½ cup orange juice

½ cup pineapple juice

½ cup white rum, preferably Bacardi

½ cup vodka

2 green apples, quartered, cored, and sliced

2 oranges, sliced

2 lemons, sliced

2 limes, sliced

1 pineapple, peeled, quartered lengthwise, cored and sliced
crosswise

Ice

Combine all ingredients except ice in a large pitcher and
refrigerate, tightly covered, for at least 12 hours. Serve with ice.

EATING

· 1 ·

The Great Leveler

*I have been trying really hard to think of some-*thing new to say about Southern food, a subject that I (along with a host of other people) have written a whole lot about.

I have written about funeral food and pimiento cheese factions and George Jones versus Jimmy Dean sausage. I have attempted to prove the superiority of Southern cuisine by the all-too-easy comparison of our Junior League cookbooks with those from the North (*Talk About Good!* versus *Posh Pantry*; Aunt Margie's Better than Sex Cake versus Grape Nuts Pudding). And I am still trying to prove the existence of the lone Mexican who introduced the hot tamale to the Mississippi Delta, where I grew up.

Whether or not this mythic figure ever actually roamed these parts is immaterial. The existence of the Delta tamale itself proves what I have long known, that Southern food is the Great Leveler. Hot tamales are beloved by rich and poor, black and white, and they are easily accessible at roadside stands, cafes, and restaurants. A dozen hots wrapped in shucks at either Scott's Hot Tamales in Greenville or the White Front Café in Rosedale sells for eight dollars. The ones wrapped in paper at Greenville's Doe's Eat Place (my own personal favorites and the first solid food I ever ate) sell for a little more than ten dollars. But then, pretty much all great Southern food is cheap. Wyatt Cooper, the late, Mississippi-born husband of Gloria Vanderbilt and father of Anderson Cooper, once wrote that, "The best French restaurants in the world are wasted on me. All I want is a few ham hocks fried in bacon grease, a little mess of turnips with sowbelly, and a hunk of cornbread and I'm happy."

If this was Cooper's menu of choice, then he was not only happy, but rich—even without Gloria. On my last trip to France, I dined at two of "the best French restaurants," L'Oustau de Baumanière in Les Baux and Le Grand Véfour in Paris, and the bill for four people at each place put me in mind of what my father once said about a particularly pricey family ski trip to Aspen: "Next year, we don't even have to go—I can get the same effect standing in a cold shower burning up thousand-dollar bills." France in July might not have been as chilly, but each *l'addition* was considerably more than the entire tab for a brunch I gave for a New Orleans debutante the weekend after I returned home. The deb in question was Lizzy Cordes, the daughter of my friend Elizabeth, and her special menu request was for an hors d'oeuvre I make consisting of a piece of bacon wrapped around a watermelon pickle and broiled. I was delighted to comply—these little bundles are not only inexpensive, they are salty and sweet and pair extremely well with the ham biscuits and pimiento cheese sandwiches I also passed around. The main course, 250 pieces of excellent fried chicken from McHardy's Chicken

& Fixin' on Broad Street, cost me exactly $240.90. Lizzy and her fellow debs had just been introduced to what passes for high society in my adopted city, but they seemed not just content but really, really happy to be munching away on some crispy chicken that cost less than a dollar per piece, and all the thank-you notes mentioned the food.

If Southern cuisine acts as a leveler by reducing the differences between race and class, the culture itself reduces the differences between—or the distinctness of—other cuisines introduced into our midst. Those Delta hot tamales bear little resemblance to Mexican hots, which, I'm pretty sure, are not bound together by lard and beef suet and, in the case of Doe's, porterhouse steak drippings. Just as deep-fried, bacon-wrapped, butterflied shrimp drenched in hot pink sweet-and-sour sauce on top of a ton of sautéed onions bears absolutely no resemblance to authentic Chinese cuisine. That particular item was my favorite thing on the menu at Henry Wong's How Joy, another Greenville mecca, and it was what I thought Chinese food tasted like until I left home for school at sixteen. Morris Lewis, a prominent wholesale grocer from Indianola, Mississippi, not only left home, he was invited to China on a trade visit just after Richard Nixon opened up the place, but he was still convinced that How Joy was the real—or at least the tastier—deal. Upon his return, Lewis said, "I've been all the way to China and I've still never tasted Chinese food as good as Henry Wong's."

Sadly, neither Henry Wong nor his shrimp is still with us, but almost all of my other favorites are very much around. And a lifetime of eating and cooking them has enabled me to come up with at least a few new things to say. For example, Southerners who put sugar in cornbread are impostors, or criminals, or both. I love skillet cornbread, fried hot water cornbread, and cornbread muffins, but to add sugar to any of them is an abomination. Which does not mean that I am a purist. I also love "Mexican Cornbread," which, much like our tamales, does not come from anywhere near Mexico, but from a cookbook called *Bayou Cuisine* put together by the Episcopal churchwomen of Indianola, Mississippi. Among its ingredients are canned cream corn, marinated cherry peppers, Wesson oil, and shredded Kraft sharp cheddar.

Its utter deliciousness brings me to another important point: there is no shame in the occasional canned or packaged ingredient. Nora Ephron put packaged onion soup mix in her justifiably famous meatloaf, and hundreds of hostesses across the South were at a complete loss when Kraft quit making its jalapeño cheese roll (most often referred to as "nippy cheese"), the key ingredient in Spinach Madeleine. The spicy spinach dish was invented by St. Francisville, Louisiana, native Madeline Wright in 1956, and when it appeared three years later in the first edition of *River Road Recipes,* published by the Junior League of Baton Rouge, it immediately put the cookbook on the map. "If there were an Academy Award for cookbooks, the Oscar for Best Performance would go hands down to *River Road Recipes,*" pronounced no less an expert than Craig Claiborne.

Then, of course, there is the mighty Ritz cracker, without which at least half my mother's entire repertoire would be decimated. She fries eggplant and green tomatoes in crushed Ritz crackers, uses them in place of bread crumbs or the lowly saltine in squash soufflés, and puts them on top of pretty much every casserole she makes, including her own now famous spinach dish, V.D. Spinach. So named because she served it to every "visiting dignitary" (from Bill and Pat Buckley to Ronald Reagan) who passed through our house, V.D. Spinach was chosen for inclusion in *The Essential New York Times Cookbook,* despite the fact that it includes frozen chopped spinach, Philadelphia cream cheese, and canned artichoke hearts.

I've also learned that Arkansas Travelers may well be the best tomatoes in the world, and all tomatoes are improved by peeling them. This latter point has been driven home to me all my life by my mother, who once peeled several hundred tomatoes for the Katrina refugees who had evacuated to Greenville's convention center as accompaniments to—what else?—fried chicken. A couple of summers ago, my friends Ben and Libby Page hosted a brunch in Nashville at which they peeled and served huge platters of various heirloom varieties alongside their collection of Irish crystal salt cellars containing various salts from around the world. This added a decidedly chic element to every Southerner's favorite summer pleasure. When I visited Ben and Libby at their Tennessee farm afterward, we had tomatoes from their garden with two or three different salts, as well as skillet corn and squash casserole, a revered summer trinity which leads me to my last point: Southerners have been doing "farm to table"—mostly by necessity—since long before the phrase was taken up by every foodie in the land.

There is a reason, after all, why Mark Twain sent a lengthy bill of fare home ahead of him after he'd spent so much time in Europe. Among the things he'd missed the most were: "Virginia bacon, broiled; . . . peach cobbler, Southern style; butter beans; sweet potatoes; green corn cut from the ear and served with butter and pepper; succotash; soft shell crabs." I am reminded again of Wyatt Cooper, as well as of the fact that pretty much the only thing I remember from my aforementioned meals in France was a side of tiny *haricots verts* just picked from L'Oustau de Baumanière's garden and drenched in fresh butter. And then there's the exchange between Katharine Ann Porter and William Faulkner that occurred at a swanky French restaurant that was probably Maxim's. They had dined well and enjoyed a fair amount of Burgundy and port, but at the end of the meal Faulkner's eyes glazed over a bit and he said, "Back home the butter beans are in, the speckled ones," to which a visibly moved Porter could only respond, "Blackberries." Now I've repeated this exchange in print at least once before, and it is hardly new, but I don't care. No matter who we are or where we've been, we are all, apparently, "leveled" by the same thing: our love of our sometimes lowly, always luscious cuisine—our love, in short, of home.

Since my own home was the site of many a festive dinner featuring V.D. Spinach, I include it below even though I've published it before. It is simply too good and too easy not to. I also include a reworked Spinach Madeleine, long a staple at my mother's holiday parties. Mama serves it in a silver chafing dish surrounded by toast points, but it's also pretty much the exact same dip that the Houston's restaurant chain serves with tortilla chips and salsa to very good effect. After Kraft killed the crucial "nippy cheese," the Junior League scrambled and posted a replacement recipe on its Web site substituting chopped fresh jalapeños and Velveeta. Word is that Madeline herself finds the Velveeta too watery and the version below features actual cheddar, plus a few of my own additions.

The squash casserole is my mother's, based on a version made by her childhood cook, Eleanor, and the blackberry cobbler, adapted from *Chez Panisse Desserts* by the brilliant Lindsey Shere, is the best I've ever had. If the blackberries are especially beautiful, I use them exclusively. But the cobbler is also delicious with a mix of blackberries, blueberries, and raspberries, which lends a patriotic touch for Memorial Day and Fourth of July celebrations.

V.D. SPINACH

(Yield: 6 to 8 servings)

1 tablespoon butter, for greasing the baking dish

Two 10-ounce packages frozen chopped spinach

½ cup butter, melted, plus 1 tablespoon butter, melted, for the topping

One 8-ounce package cream cheese, softened

1 teaspoon fresh lemon juice

One 14-ounce can artichoke hearts, drained and halved

1 cup coarse Ritz cracker crumbs

Preheat the oven to 350 degrees. Butter a shallow 2-quart casserole.

Cook the spinach according to the package directions. Drain well, pressing hard against the strainer or colander to get as much water as possible out. Place in a mixing bowl and add the ½ cup of melted butter, the cream cheese, and the lemon juice and mix well.

Place the artichoke heart halves evenly over the bottom of the casserole. Cover with the spinach mixture and smooth the top.

Cover the top with the Ritz crumbs, drizzle with 1 tablespoon (or more if needed) of melted butter, and bake on the middle rack until bubbly in the center and lightly browned on the top, about 25 minutes.

SPINACH MADELEINE

(*Yield: 6 to 8 servings*)

2 packages frozen chopped spinach

4 tablespoons butter

2 tablespoons flour

½ cup evaporated milk

¼ cup finely chopped onion

2 teaspoons finely chopped jalapeño peppers

1 cup sharp cheddar cheese, grated

2 garlic cloves, pressed

1 teaspoon Worcestershire sauce

1½ teaspoons salt

½ teaspoon black pepper

1 pinch cayenne pepper

Cook spinach according to directions on the package. Drain and reserve ½ cup of the liquor.

Melt the butter in a saucepan over low heat. Whisk in flour until blended and smooth but not brown. Add onions and cook until soft. Slowly add milk and spinach liquor, stirring constantly to avoid lumps. Continue stirring and cook until smooth and thick.

Add remaining ingredients to the white sauce and stir until the cheese has melted. Taste for seasonings—you may want more heat in the form of the chopped jalapeño and/or cayenne, as well as more salt.

NOTE: This may be served immediately, as a side dish or a dip. If the latter, you may want to double the recipe, place in a chafing dish, and surround with toast points. Or, it can be placed in a buttered casserole or gratin dish and topped with buttered bread crumbs, or a mixture of buttered bread crumbs and grated Parmesan cheese. Put the dish in a 350-degree oven until the crumbs are brown.

JUDY'S SQUASH CASSEROLE

(*Yield: 8 servings*)

8 yellow crookneck squash, about 2½ to 3 pounds

8 tablespoons (1 stick) butter, plus 1 tablespoon for greasing casserole and 3 tablespoons for topping

1 sweet onion, finely chopped

½ teaspoon sugar

1 teaspoon salt

½ teaspoon freshly ground black pepper

¼ teaspoon dried basil

2 hard-boiled eggs

⅓ cup sour cream

⅓ cup heavy cream

1 sleeve Ritz crackers

Preheat the oven to 350 degrees. Butter a shallow 2-quart baking dish.

Scrub and trim squash and slice thickly. Place slices in the bowl of a food processor, and process until diced fairly finely. (You will likely have to do this in at least two batches.)

Melt butter in large heavy skillet and sauté onion until translucent. Add squash, sugar, salt, pepper, and basil. Cook until squash is tender and transfer to a large mixing bowl.

Push eggs through a sieve and add to squash with sour cream and heavy cream. Mix well.

Crush crackers. (You don't want to get them too fine—the easiest way to do it is to roll up the cracker sleeves in a dish towel and pound with a rolling pin.) Melt 3 tablespoons butter and toss with crumbs. Pour squash mixture into baking dish, top with the buttered crumbs, and bake for about 45 minutes, until the squash is bubbling and the topping is nice and brown.

THE BEST BLACKBERRY COBBLER

(*Yield: 6 to 8 servings*)

4½ cups blackberries

⅓ cup sugar

1 tablespoon flour

FOR THE BISCUIT TOPPING

1½ cups flour

⅜ teaspoon salt

1½ tablespoons sugar

2¼ teaspoons baking powder

6 tablespoons unsalted butter

¾ cup whipping cream

Preheat the oven to 375 degrees.

Toss berries with the sugar and flour and set aside. (If the berries are especially juicy, add another half tablespoon of flour.)

Mix the dry ingredients for the biscuit dough. (If you use salted butter, add only a pinch of salt.) Cut in the butter with two forks or a pastry blender until it looks like coarse cornmeal. (You may also use a food processor.) Add the cream and mix lightly until the mixture is just moistened.

Put the berries in a 1½ quart gratin or baking dish. Make patties of the dough about 2½ inches in diameter and ½ inch thick. Arrange them over the top of the berries. Bake for 40 to 45 minutes until the topping is brown and the berry juices bubble around it.

· 2 ·

The Society Diet

*In Nan Kempner's coffee-table book on enter-*taining, *R.S.V.P.,* there is a luncheon menu from Marie-Chantal, the wife of Crown Princess Pavlos of Greece. It consists of: a soup made of grapefruit juice with pureed cucumber, celery, and tomato; a soufflé made with low-fat cheese, no butter, six egg whites, and only two egg yolks; and "individual lemon tarts" that are devoid of pastry crusts and billed as "no-guilt sweet treats." In the photographs, the hostess and her guests are all very stylish and very skinny, and the French chef who dreamed up the "spa menu" is especially attractive. But the whole thing brings to mind Ruth Draper's priceless monologue "Diets and Doctors," in which a woman and her three guests get a much-coveted table at an extremely fashionable restaurant and they each turn out to be on a rigid diet. The hostess/Draper character must then ask the French waiter for such off-the-menu items as a single cold, boiled turnip ("Will you make it your personal choice and serve it attractively?"), raw carrots ("Just wash them, she wants the whole bunch"), and the juice of eleven lemons ("She's on the one hundred lemon cure.... What courage!"). She then trumps them all by ordering nothing for herself ("No thanks, I don't take anything").

Now, in these days of routine juicing, cleansing, and all-vegan, gluten-free diets, Draper's monologue has morphed from send-up to borderline serious, and I feel sure that Marie-Chantal's guests were all of like minds (except for their children, who were allowed to eat spaghetti). But in general, I have a thing about hosts imposing their diet regimens on their guests, and about guests who make outrageous requests that don't have anything to do with a life-threatening condition. (This may well come from the fact that when I was in boarding school at Madeira, in Virginia, outside of Washington, D.C., the headmistress, Jean Harris, put the entire, already culinarily deprived student body on the Scarsdale Diet. We did not know until she subsequently shot and killed Dr. Herman Tarnower in his bed that she had been romantically involved with the diet's creator.)

Revlon founder Charles Revson's dinner was invariably a single can of water packed tuna unmolded on a plate. If he were dining out, his chauffeur would deliver one to his hosts in the afternoon. After one of then Vice President Dick Cheney's heart episodes, I attended a dinner at the British Embassy and noticed that Cheney was served a plate of pineapple and blueberries for dessert while the rest of us got a gooey chocolate mousse. The embassy's social director told me later that the kitchen had made the choice for him, to be thoughtful, so we'll never know for sure if that's what he really wanted. I'm betting not, but then I'm a big believer in free will at the table—something that has occasionally been in short supply in Washington, particularly at the White House.

In *FDR, A Centenary Remembrance,* Joe Alsop, the columnist who was a cousin of both Franklin and Eleanor Roosevelt, as well as a great gourmand, writes that Eleanor "had imported a nutritionist to be the presidential housekeeper, and year after year this woman showed that nutritionists may well know how to make food healthful, but scorn to make it appetizing or even edible. The salads were especially deplorable . . . and might even conceal bits of marshmallow in their dreadful depths." It was so bad, reports Alsop, that Martha Gellhorn, invited to dinner along with her fiancé Ernest Hemingway, ate a plateful of sandwiches prior to the party— "nor was she the only precautionary sandwich-eater among those accustomed to the White House cuisine . . . I suspected then that this extreme Puritanism about food in a house whose master liked to eat well . . . was another manifestation of Eleanor Roosevelt's detestation of anything savoring of worldly ways. She equated plain living with high thinking, so it was moral to eat badly."

As it happens, the chicest, thinnest people always seem to serve the best, most luxurious food. My maternal grandmother, who was a frequent guest at Elizabeth Arden's Maine Chance Beauty Spa, could live for weeks on some combination of jellied consommé, gin, and cottage cheese. But on the cook's night off, she always made my grandfather creamed chicken on toast, one of the two things she knew how to make. (The other, made with similar amounts of butter and cream, was a delicious hot chocolate sauce.) During the Duchess of Windsor's first marriage, she was too poor to hire a cook, so she taught herself from the fairly hearty Fannie

Farmer's *Boston Cooking-School Cook Book*. Even after she married the Prince of Wales she was known to serve fried chicken, and included a recipe for it in her own book, *Some Favorite Southern Recipes of the Duchess of Windsor*, whose proceeds from its sales went toward the war effort. Renowned hostess Pat Buckley once told me she thought of her typical ladies lunch entrée of "filet of sole or soft shell crabs meunière," as light fare. When I pointed out that both dishes are swimming in butter, she said, "Well, I don't serve them salads. I like to think of myself as a purveyor of good food." The rail-thin Buckley also professed not to be able to live without two desserts a day, nor could she imagine a soufflé without cream or butter. "They don't taste like anything."

The great fashion designer Bill Blass might have made clothes for "social x-rays," but he made a point of serving what he called "real American food" like corn fritters, pineapple upside-down cake, and the meatloaf that became his signature. A 1970s ad for his perfume featured a list of his "likes" and "dislikes" with regard to women, and the first entry in the "dislikes" column was "A woman who talks about dieting all the time." The first time I had lunch with him, in the Grill Room at the Four Seasons, he chastised the waiter for being chintzy with the white truffle he shaved over our fettuccine. At my last lunch with Blass, in his Connecticut country house just a month or so before he died, we had an heirloom tomato salad with red onion and purple basil, along with a heaping platter of egg salad sandwiches, salami sandwiches, and roast beef and Brie sandwiches, accompanied by his favorite sweet pickled green tomatoes.

Sadly, too many hosts and hostesses are not nearly as adept (or fearless) as Blass and Buckley and they end up putting their guests on a sort of accidental diet. After Evangeline Bruce's husband died, she took to entertaining via regular Sunday brunches—except that they weren't really brunches at all, but stand-up midday cocktail parties with entirely un-appetizing things like plain, hard-boiled quails' eggs passed on trays decorated with enormous "nests" of seaweed. In Sally Quinn's book *The Party,* she recalls one of these affairs at which poor Princess Margaret kept knocking back bourbon and refusing what she took to be the "hors d'oeuvres" in favor of the sit-down meal that never came—much to the distress of her increasingly nervous escort.

After the Princess Margaret episode, Quinn's husband, Ben Bradlee, refused to attend any more of Bruce's midday parties, which is actually more polite than going and refusing what is offered. Since ancient times, food has been "the symbol of fellowship with the host," writes Margaret Visser in *The Rituals of Dinner.* "To refuse food is to reject the fellowship, and also to prevent the host from playing the hostly role, which is to confer honor." Visser quotes one Baronne Staffe, who is especially firm on the subject. "If dishes are failures you do not notice. You eat bravely what is offered as if it were good." Baronne Staffe's example of a perfect guest is "a heroic Frenchman visiting England who drank . . . and pronounced excellent a 'frightful beverage' offered to him as a rare wine," only to learn that he had been served medicine by mistake.

Winston Churchill was once served a Tom Collins on pur-pose by Franklin Roosevelt's cousin Laura Delano, and, in the middle of a serious conversation with FDR (this was 1942), turned and spit it out. Churchill refused to drink much of any-thing but Johnnie Walker Red, brandy, gin, and Pol Roger champagne, but he did save the free world, and, therefore, could pretty much do whatever he wanted. Anyway, according to Erasmus, it is perfectly acceptable to spit something out, although he does recommend withdrawing first. "Vomiting is not shameful, but to have vomited through gluttony is disgusting." Once, a guest at my house, a friend of a friend from Los Angeles, vomited on ethical grounds. She had just enthusiastically finished her second helping of the Creole dish Grillades and Grits, when she learned that the "grillades" were veal and she couldn't bear the knowledge that a baby cow had been slaughtered for her supper. I thought her reaction a bit extreme, but apologized profusely for not alerting her earlier as to the dish's contents. After all, another of Erasmus's rules is that "the essence of good manners consists in freely pardoning the shortcomings of others although nowhere near falling short yourself."

BILL BLASS'S MEATLOAF

(*Yield: 6 servings*)

4 tablespoons butter

1 cup chopped celery

1 cup chopped onion

2 pounds ground sirloin

½ pound ground pork

½ pound ground veal

½ cup minced parsley

1½ cups fresh bread crumbs

1 egg, beaten, with 1 tablespoon Worcestershire sauce

½ cup sour cream

1 tablespoon heavy cream

1 teaspoon salt

Freshly ground black pepper, to taste

1 pinch each of dried thyme and dried marjoram

One 12-ounce bottle of Heinz Chili Sauce

5 strips bacon

Preheat the oven to 350 degrees.

Melt butter in a skillet over medium heat and sauté celery and onion, stirring frequently, until soft and translucent. In a large bowl, combine with the meats, parsley, bread crumbs, and egg mixture. (The only way to do this effectively is with your hands.) Combine the sour cream and heavy cream and fold in. Add seasonings. Place in a 5 × 9-inch loaf pan or shape into a loaf of roughly the same dimensions and place on a rimmed baking dish. Cover the top with chili sauce and lay strips of bacon across. Bake for 1 hour.

NOTE: When I was growing up, our family's beloved cook, Lottie Martin, made a meatloaf very similar to Bill's. But she added ½ cup of brown sugar to the chili sauce slathered on the top. I wish I'd remembered to tell Bill that—I think he would have loved it. Since I know he loved cream, I've followed a tip from Blackberry Farm's Sam Beall and added a touch of both sour and heavy cream to keep things moist.

JULIA BROOKS'S CHICKEN HASH

(*Yield: 4 to 6 servings*)

3 tablespoons butter

1 small onion, chopped

¼ cup celery (preferably the tender inner stalks, including leaves) chopped

½ cup thick sliced white mushrooms

Worcestershire sauce

Salt

Freshly ground black pepper

1½ tablespoons flour

1 cup heavy cream (or half cream and half chicken stock)

2 cups cooked chicken cut into 1-inch square pieces

Melt 2 tablespoons of the butter in skillet over medium-low heat. Add chopped onion and celery and cook until soft. While the vegetables are cooking, melt the remaining tablespoon of butter in a small skillet and quickly sauté the mushrooms, adding salt and pepper and a dash or two of Worcestershire sauce. Set aside.

Sprinkle the flour into the skillet with the softened onion and celery, stirring constantly. Slowly add cream, still stirring constantly, until it is completely incorporated and the sauce is a bit thick. Add the cooked chicken and mushrooms and salt and pepper to taste.

NOTE: Brooke Astor made a similar dish called Chicken Hash October, published in a 1946 edition of *Vogue* and so-named, she said, "because October is my cooking month. The maids come to town and we stay in the country and do all our own cooking." Clearly, chicken hash was the staple of otherwise spoiled ladies forced to do without their help. Mrs. Astor spooned her hash onto squares of crisp toast and garnished each serving with "crisply cooked bacon" and parsley sprigs, which sound to me like excellent additions.

· 3 ·

Dining on the Nile

Among the most beloved items in my increasingly crowded office are: a big and very-early-twentieth-century photograph of waves crashing at Colombo, Sri Lanka; a nineteenth-century map of Africa and a Masai beaded bag on a stand; mounted and framed specimens of Julia butterflies given to me by my husband on my birthday; a brilliantly colored *suzani* from Afghanistan; and two framed postcards from the Victoria and Albert Museum. One is a reproduction of a seventeenth-century Indian watercolor of an absinthe green magpie against a saffron yellow background, and the other is a photograph of a seemingly spent dinner table on a houseboat cruising down the Nile. In the latter, the table is covered in a linen tablecloth and set with gold-rimmed Old Paris plates, weighty silver forks and spoons, and an assortment of glass beakers, champagne flutes, and wineglasses. An earthenware water jug, a pair of silver candlesticks, a bottle of claret, and another of champagne also litter the table, above which hangs an Indian glass lantern.

On the walls, there's a William Daniels print, a satchel on a hook, and a pair of gilded mirrors.

I've put myself in that cabin and imagined myself at that table more times than I can count, but it's only one of the treasures described above that can take me to other worlds— ones where I've already been or where I long to go.

Webster's defines the word exotic as "strikingly, excitingly, or mysteriously unusual or different." In the case of some of my own exotic images, there's also a strong element of nostalgia. I can't pull up to the table on that boat any more than I can explore India during the Raj. But I find it inspiring to be surrounded by the relics of the curiosity of those who came before me, and I'm often catapulted out of my chair—either to the bookshelf across the room where I can read about the exploits of others, or further down the road where I can enjoy some of my own.

As much as I love to be in London, my favorite city, or Spain, where I am constantly pulled, it's those "excitingly different" and often supremely uncomfortable places that I recall most vividly. And, of course, I remember what I ate there. There was the rich consommé that was pretty much the only consumable thing on the Trans-Siberian railway to Novosibirsk (other than beer and vodka), followed by mounds of caviar in Moscow, to which I'd returned via a terrifyingly ancient Aeroflot plane. There was the picnic of cold roast chicken and Tusker beer beside Tanzania's Mara River, where the hooves of antelopes—recent bounty of the leopard who'd dragged them up the branches of a massive fig tree—tinkled above us like so many wind chimes. There were the cherries picked alongside Gypsies in the Romanian countryside just after the Ceauşescus had been executed, and the mojitos at an illegal jazz club in Havana, where the Cuban equivalent of Tina Turner gyrated like crazy and the bass player's stand-up instrument was held together by glue and wire.

Finally, there was the inn in Kabul where the British manager's perfect gin and tonics and astonishingly sophisticated fare made it easier to ignore the scorpions scuttling in our rooms.

I'd gone to Afghanistan in 2003 to write about a fledgling beauty school. During the Taliban's regime, it was illegal for women to work, but many risked their lives to run clandestine salons in their houses, often hiding their supplies by burying them in their backyards. Curling hair, even with perm rods crudely carved out of wood, was one of the very few ways they could support their families and maintain some self-esteem. Now they wanted to perfect their skills and open up their own small businesses.

The women in the school had only recently shed their burkas and they looked forward to the daily midday break as a long denied opportunity to socialize. Lunch was prepared by Naija, whose husband had been paralyzed by a land mine, and every day brought a literally fresh revelation. Who knew that the eggplant and tomatoes that were the chief ingredients of my new favorite dish *buranee banjan* could thrive in the middle of a giant dust bowl? There was not a lot of visible commerce going on—except for the produce stands on almost every block. If it hadn't been for the tear-inducing exhaust, you could have smelled the bundles of mint and cilantro stacked next to the ubiquitous bags of dried chickpeas. Just outside the school, a man appeared every morning with a wagon full of *kharboza,* a white-fleshed watermelon that is possibly the best thing I've ever tasted.

Dinners at the Gandamack Lodge, located in a house once rented by Osama bin Laden's fourth wife, were even more of a surprise. Owned by Peter Juvenal, a BBC cameraman and an old Afghan hand, it was managed at the time by a Sloaney but intrepid young Brit named Jamie Peck. The twenty-odd guests shared some bare-bones bathrooms, and the scorpions were indeed alarming, but there was not a lot Jamie could do about either of those things. What he did do was keep the place well stocked with booze and wine and very cold beer and create a menu that was breathtakingly ambitious given our environs. On our third night, a guard was killed in a robbery at a similar nearby guesthouse, but once inside the Gandamack's gates, we turned into Graham Greene characters, gin-soaked and willfully oblivious to the danger all around us.

Jamie had managed to locate a sixty-something-year-old chef named Noor, who had been unemployed since the Soviets invaded in 1979. More than twenty years on, Noor, like most of his countrymen, had all but lost his skills, but Jamie, with his limited Dari and unlimited enthusiasm, coaxed them out of him. The unlikely partnership resulted in some seriously good food: chilled cucumber soup with dill, spit-roasted leg of lamb, a lemon curd tart, fish cakes accompanied by a tangy chili jam. On our last night, the menu included some particularly ingenious risotto cakes with a little ball of mozzarella buried inside that melted when they were cooked.

I make those cakes a lot—they're a perfect dinner-party first course because most of the work can be done well ahead of time (unlike regular risotto) and they look really pretty napped with a simple tomato sauce. Sometimes I add a half cup of chopped prosciutto that's been sautéed in a bit of olive oil to the risotto; sometimes I make like Noor and throw in a pinch of saffron and bits of braised artichoke hearts (dice about six fresh artichoke hearts, sauté them in a little butter and water until the liquid's gone and add them with the onion). Either way, they are delicious and they always remind me of my decidedly exotic sojourn to a little piece of paradise in an otherwise war-ravaged country. Those civilized, almost otherworldly evenings at the Gandamack are likely the closest I'll ever come to dinner on that houseboat on the Nile.

RISOTTO CAKES WITH MOZZARELLA

(*Yield: About 15 cakes or 7 servings*)

5 cups chicken stock

7 tablespoons butter

10 tablespoons olive oil

1 medium onion, finely chopped

2 cups Arborio rice

½ cup freshly grated Parmesan cheese, plus more for serving

½ pound fresh mozzarella

2 to 3 eggs

1 cup all-purpose flour

1½ cups fine day-old bread crumbs, preferably from a baguette

¼ teaspoon salt

Homemade tomato sauce, for serving

Fresh marjoram sprigs for garnish.

Bring stock to a slow simmer. Put 1 tablespoon butter,
2 tablespoons olive oil, and the onion in a heavy saucepan
over medium-high heat. Stir until onion becomes translucent,
about 7 minutes. Add rice and stir to coat well. Add ½ cup of
the stock, stirring constantly, until almost all the liquid is
absorbed. Repeat process, stirring constantly, and adjust heat
so mixture simmers but rice does not scorch. After about
20 minutes, nearly all of the stock should be absorbed. Rice
should be creamy but firm to the bite. Stir in Parmesan and
2 tablespoons butter.

Remove from heat, spread risotto onto a large plate and
place in refrigerator for ½ hour until firm and chilled. Using a
spoon or a melon scooper, make 15 small half balls of the
mozzarella. Pack risotto into ⅓-cup measuring cup and invert
onto the palm of your hand. Place a half ball of mozzarella in
center and press risotto around the ball to make a patty about
2½ inches in diameter and ¾ inch thick. Make sure risotto
covers the cheese. Repeat until you have 15 rice cakes.

Place 2 eggs and 2 tablespoons water in a bowl and beat with
a fork. Spread flour and bread crumbs on separate plates. Mix salt
into bread crumbs. Coat each cake lightly with flour, dip in egg
mixture, shake off excess and coat evenly with bread crumbs. (If
needed, beat remaining egg with 1 tablespoon water.)

Preheat the oven to 200 degrees. Line a baking sheet with
paper towels. In a large skillet over medium-high heat, melt
2 tablespoons butter in 4 tablespoons oil. When butter stops

bubbling, fry the first batch of cakes until golden brown and crispy, about 2 minutes per side. Place on baking sheet and put in the oven. Drain off oil and wipe out pan with paper towels. Fry the rest of the cakes in remaining oil and butter.

To serve: Place two cakes on each plate. Sprinkle with Parmesan and spoon tomato sauce around them. Garnish with marjoram.

Tomato Sauce

(*Yield: 2 cups*)

2 pounds ripe plum tomatoes or 2 cups canned tomatoes
    and their juice

5 tablespoons butter

1 medium yellow onion, peeled and halved

1½ teaspoons salt

¼ teaspoon sugar

1 tablespoon fresh marjoram, finely chopped, or 1 teaspoon
    dried

If using fresh tomatoes, cut them in half lengthwise and put them in a covered heavy-bottomed pot. Bring to a simmer and cook for 10 minutes.

Puree the tomatoes through a food mill and put back into pot. Add the butter, onion, salt, and sugar. Cook at a slow but steady simmer, uncovered, for 30 minutes. Add the marjoram and cook for 10 or 15 minutes more. Remove onion and taste for salt.

BURANEE BANJAN

(*Yield: 8 servings*)

4 medium eggplants (about 1 pound each)

Salt

6 tablespoons olive oil

3 medium onions, finely chopped

2 large ripe tomatoes, peeled, seeded, and sliced
  (or 4 or 5 large plum tomatoes)

¼ teaspoon cayenne pepper or to taste

Yogurt sauce (recipe below)

A handful of fresh mint, finely chopped or torn

Nan or lavash bread for serving

Preheat the broiler. Remove the stems from eggplant and cut
crosswise into ½-inch slices. Select the 24 best slices (not the
puffy ends) and discard the rest. Sprinkle slices liberally with
salt, leave for 30 minutes, then dry well.

Brush slices with 2 tablespoons of the olive oil and arrange
on cookie sheets. Broil until lightly browned, 2 to 3 minutes per
side. (Don't cook the slices completely.)

In a deep 12-inch skillet, over medium heat, sauté the
onions in 4 tablespoons of olive oil for 15 minutes, until a deep
reddish brown—but not crisp. Remove to a plate with a slotted
spoon.

Place 8 rounds of eggplant into the same skillet. Top with half of the chopped onion and tomato slices. Mix 1 teaspoon salt and the cayenne and sprinkle one-third over the tomatoes. Repeat with another layer of eggplant and the remaining onions and tomatoes. Sprinkle another third of the remaining cayenne mixture. Place an eggplant slice on top of each stack and sprinkle with remaining cayenne. Add ¼ cup water and cover skillet tightly. Simmer about 30 minutes.

To serve: Spread half the yogurt sauce onto the bottom of a serving dish. Top with the vegetables, lifting stacks carefully. Top with the remainder of the yogurt, and drizzle with pan juices. Sprinkle generously with mint. Serve immediately, with nan or lavash.

YOGURT SAUCE
(*Yield: 2 cups*)

2 cups plain whole milk yogurt

2 garlic cloves, peeled and crushed or pushed through a
    garlic press

Pinch of salt

Place yogurt in cheesecloth or a muslin-lined strainer and drain over a bowl for 1 hour. Mix with garlic and salt to taste.

· 4 ·

Lady in Spain

Several years ago I packed up a bag of books and a bag of clothes and took off for Spain. I had never just taken off before, not as a student, not in my early twenties like most of my friends, not ever (unless you count a handful of lost weekends in college when, under the influence of lust and other stimulants, I disappeared to Maine). I went, ostensibly, to learn Spanish—my Presbyterian upbringing wouldn't allow me to classify such an extended trip as pure escape, so I came up with an actual reason to go. Also, since two-thirds of the Western Hemisphere speaks the language, I figured it wouldn't be a bad thing to do. (In school, I'd chosen sophistication over practicality and studied the French I barely remember.)

So I found an apartment off Madrid's Plaza Mayor and paid a big pile of euros to a language school run, improbably, by an Irish vegetarian named Declan, who was appalled at my love of bullfights and the huge Spanish rib steaks (*chuletóns*) sprinkled with coarse salt from Restaurant Alkalde (not to mention the strip steaks brought sizzling to the table at Casa

Paco or at the very happening Lucio, around the corner.) Declan tried hard, but I never learned proper Spanish. Instead I ate and drank, making dozens of trips to the Prado and attending the bullfights every night during the feria. I learned the difference between *gambas* and *cigalas* and *carabineros* (three of the heavenly sea creatures available *a la plancha*, simply cooked on a griddle, at the glorious La Trainera); I communed, a lot, with Angel, the aptly named maitre d'hotel at El Lando, my favorite restaurant in all of Madrid.

I did learn some Spanish, but it was a very specific kind. *Panuelo*, for example, means handkerchief, as in the white (*blanco*) one thrown out by the president of the bullfight to signal its start, or the very rare orange (*naranja*) one, held up to save the life of an especially brave bull. *Bellotas* are the acorns fed to the hogs that make the most tender—and most expensive—pork roasts and hams. If you want a couple of olives in your martini, you must ask for *aceitunes* rather than *olivos*, which usually are olive trees. (The expression *tamar el olivo* means "to have the olive tree"—to jump or climb it very quickly. This is also used when a bull gets after a *banderillero* and he swings himself equally quickly over the fence and out of the ring.) And if you want a drink during the bullfights you must yell "*cerveza, por favor*" or "*whisky con hielo*," because beer and Scotch are the only alcohol sold in the stands. I may not have earned a certificate from Declan's school, but I picked up loads of knowledge that to me, at least, is far more useful.

My guides in a great many of my endeavors were Jenny and Juan Luis Hernandez Miron. Jenny grew up in the Arkansas Delta, just across the river from where I was born. She met Juan Luis, a professor, more than twenty years ago, during a college year abroad in Madrid, married him two years later, and she's been there ever since. Juan Luis spent eleven years writing the definitive Spanish-Greek dictionary; he has had season tickets to the Madrid bullfights for more than thirty years. He is the kind of guy who, on no notice, can somehow procure the only five tickets to a bullfight to be had during Seville's crowded feria, even on the day that the wildly popular José Tomás is fighting—and he'll also know the best place (Barbiana) to have lunch beforehand. Jenny is as entertaining and fun-loving as Juan Luis, and at least as useful since she speaks fluent Spanish, French, and Italian (Juan Luis doesn't exactly speak English).

One of our first treks together was to Plasencia, Juan Luis's hometown in the Extremadura region. Though he has visited Jenny's and my homeland countless times (I'm pretty sure he's the only Spaniard who has made repeat trips to both Portland, Arkansas and Greenville, Mississippi), I had never seen his. Also, he'd been trying to explain to me the difference between pure Spanish paprika and that of Hungary or South American countries (the tasteless stuff sold by American spice companies is not even worth mentioning), so he was adamant that I visit his uncle's *pimentón* factory in Aldeanueva del Camino, a town in La Vera, the northern part of Extremadura. Pimentón de la Vera, with its unique smoky-sweet taste, is regarded as the finest paprika in Spain.

On the drive west from Madrid we passed literally hundreds of storks (*las ciguenas*), nesting, in what appear to be impossible feats of balance and engineering (these nests are enormous), on the points of church steeples and bell towers, on the apexes and outer corners of roofs, at the tops of electrical towers and construction cranes. (The storks have ruined so many rooftops that the government placed specially designed, elevated steel structures on top of the roofs they seemed most fond of, but the storks simply built their nests underneath them.) We looked up at the house on a hill where Franco and the young Juan Carlos had their secret meeting to discuss Franco's plan for the boy to become king upon his death, as well as his education in the meantime. And in Plasencia we walked by the house on the cobbled street where Juan Luis grew up, and to the bar where he is still warmly embraced—but where, alas, they were sold out of the pork-and-paprika tapa he remembered so fondly.

The next day though, we saw plenty of paprika at Pimentón Santo Domingo, founded in 1908, and owned by Mariano Miron, a former schoolteacher and mayor of the town. The outside of the building is painted the paprika red and deep sky blue as the chic paprika can—I took a big one home to adorn my kitchen. Inside, not a thing appears to be changed since the day the first peppers were ground. The grinding takes place in an enormous Rube Goldberg contraption that extends over two floors and features a complicated set of pipes going in and out of windows, connecting bins and grinders and a giant sieve that looks like a pinball machine. It was all a bit too much for me to take in, but basically, the peppers are first dumped into a machine that takes off the stem (el pezón, "the nipple"), and they are then, seeds and all, funneled into another machine where they are crushed between two ancient-looking stone wheels. By the time it's all over, each batch goes through a fine grinder at least six times, and finally through the sieve, where it runs down in troughs into big bags, collected on wooden carts and rolled away.

The grinding takes place from October to January or February, and even though I didn't visit until May, a fine red dust still covered everything. The only "equipment" besides the grinding apparatus are straw bags used to tote the peppers (the same ones that the blood-stained dust of the bullring is swept into during breaks in the action), the painted wooden carts, and tables where the paprika is scooped into tins and marked *dulce*, *agridulce*, or *picante*. The *dulce*, or sweet, the most widely used, is made with a round pepper called *la bola*. Both *agridulce* and *picante* are made from a longer, thinner red pepper with a bit more bite, but *picante* is given heat by adding cayenne.

When we left, Uncle Mariano plied us with tins of all three, and the taste was a revelation. Up to that point, I think I'd only ever sprinkled paprika on top of stuffed eggs or over bowls of potato salad to make them pretty—there was no point in using it to flavor anything since the flavor most closely approximated red sawdust. But this tasted like actual sweet and sweet-hot peppers that had been dried using smoke. In Spain, paprika is used to flavor everything from chorizo (the sausage that takes a lot) to garlic soup (which takes a pinch).

It is also used in a variety of marinades for lamb or pork, or in the simpler tapa Juan Luis had hoped to order in his old haunt in Plasencia. Back in Madrid, he made it for us. First he sliced three onions and two tenderloins of pork very thin. Next he heated about 2 tablespoons of olive oil in a skillet, added the onions, and sweated them, covered, for about five minutes before adding a half teaspoon of *picante* paprika and cooking for two or three minutes more. Finally he layered the pork slices on top, poured about a half cup of dry sherry over them and turned up the heat. In five minutes he turned the slices and cooked them until they were a golden brown on the bottom. Then he served the pork, without the onion, sprinkled with sea salt and lemon, along with slices of baguette. The dish is Spanish cooking at its simple, elegant best. Below, I offer a similar, more substantial version that I serve as a main course accompanied by rice (preferably cooked in chicken stock with a thread or two of saffron) and a classic pisto (as opposed to the French pistou) taught to me by a waiter at Casa Paco, where it is not to be missed.

PORK LOIN MARINATED IN PAPRIKA AND HERBS

(*Yield: 4 to 6 servings*)

5 garlic cloves

¼ cup minced fresh oregano leaves

1 tablespoon imported sweet paprika

2 teaspoons fresh thyme leaves

1 teaspoon salt or to taste

1 teaspoon freshly ground black pepper

5 tablespoons olive oil, plus more for cooking

1 tablespoon red-wine vinegar

1¼ pounds boneless pork loin, cut into 1½-inch pieces or 1 whole tenderloin.

Crush the garlic with a press or in a mortar. Add the remaining ingredients, except the pork, and make into a paste. Toss the cubed pork with the paste in a bowl or smear onto the whole tenderloin. Marinate in the refrigerator for at least 24 hours.

Coat a large skillet with olive oil and heat until smoking. If using the whole tenderloin, slice it into ½-inch slices. Add slices or cubes to the skillet and brown on all sides. Reduce the heat to medium and cook until just done, 10 to 15 minutes. Taste, and add more salt if necessary.

PISTO

(*Yield: 6 to 8 servings*)

3 tablespoons olive oil

4 garlic cloves, chopped

2 medium yellow onions, chopped

2 pounds zucchini, cut into ¾-inch cubes

2½ pounds tomatoes, peeled, seeded, and chopped (or the equivalent of canned diced tomatoes, about 1 large and 1 small can)

½ teaspoon sugar or to taste

1 teaspoon salt or to taste

½ teaspoon freshly ground black pepper or to taste

2 eggs, lightly beaten.

Heat the olive oil in a large skillet over medium heat. Add the garlic and onions and cook until soft, about 7 minutes. Stir in the zucchini, tomatoes, sugar, salt, and pepper. After about 5 minutes, add ¼ cup water and simmer, stirring often, mashing down on the vegetables as they soften. (A potato masher is useful.) Add more water if it cooks out before the vegetables are soft.

When the vegetables are done and the mixture resembles a chunky puree, taste and adjust the seasoning if necessary. Add the eggs, stirring quickly to incorporate, and remove from heat.

· 5 ·

Kill That Taste!

For years my friend the writer Elaine Shannon and I joked that one day we would write a cookbook called *Kill That Taste!* The idea was born from the fact that the refrigerator in Elaine's Washington, D.C., kitchen is filled almost exclusively with powerful condiments: lime pickle, an extensive collection of chutneys and relishes, capers, caperberries, mustards, and, because she is a good Georgia girl, a vast array of hot sauces. The idea was that anything accompanied by one or some combination of the above would be made better, or at the very least, unrecognizable. Even—or especially—foods people hate.

Now there are very few things I don't like, but employing our theory, I have made uninteresting things taste far livelier. The ever-present mini-bottle of Tabasco in my purse has gotten me through more airplane meals and rubber chicken dinners that I can count. It is also possible, of course, to go the opposite route and kill things with kindness. I have seen many a timid eater overcome his or her aversion to some despised food or other when it is plied with enough cream and butter. Or if it is simply fried.

Okra is an excellent case in point. I grew up eating okra at least two or three times a week and I agree with the poet and novelist James Dickey. "You talk of supping with the gods," he wrote in *Jericho*. "You've just done it, for who but a god could come up with the divine fact of okra?" Alas, we are in the minority. I suspect that many people's problem with okra is the slimy mass it becomes if you cook it too long (I don't even mind it that way, which is how you get it in school cafeterias and at inferior diners where they serve it out of cans). But frying it (slicing it, rolling it in seasoned fine white cornmeal, and frying it in about a half inch of oil or bacon grease until it's golden brown) solves the problem. Gloriously crunchy, distinctly unslimy, fried okra is as addictive as McDonald's French fries were when they were still fried in all that bad beef tallow. But you don't even have to be bad. Pan-frying the okra in a bit of olive oil and water or just steaming it until it's barely tender is just as effective in dealing with the slime quotient, and here you can indulge in a bit of Killing That Taste! I serve steamed okra at cocktail parties with a dipping sauce of curried mayonnaise or a mayo enlivened by some pressed garlic and a healthy squirt of Thai chili paste. In *Country Weekends*, the great Lee Bailey accompanies steamed okra with a wonderful tomato vinaigrette.

So few people eat okra (more radishes are grown in this country) that it never even makes it on to the lists of Top 10 hated foods. This is not the case for the perennial winners broccoli and Brussels sprouts. No less than a sitting American president (George H. W. Bush) publicly declared his distaste for broccoli; in Britain a recent poll found that broccoli is the second most hated food on the island, topped only by Brussels sprouts. That is too bad, because, like okra, which is very high in fiber, broccoli and Brussels sprouts are extremely good for you. Brussels sprouts are rich in vitamins A and C, they are a great source of potassium, thiamine, and iron, and are proven to stimulate the digestive system. Broccoli is also rich in A and C, and a study from Johns Hopkins shows that it possesses a compound that appears to be more effective than antibiotics against the bacteria that causes peptic ulcers. Even more impressive, tests in mice suggest that the same compound could offer "formidable protection" against stomach cancer, the second most common form of cancer in the world.

It would behoove us then to get munching. Whatever else their problems, I bet the ancient Romans were not beset with stomach ulcers. According to the historian Alexis Soyer, the first-century gourmet Apicius, who wrote the nearest thing to a cookbook that survives today, was so good at cooking broccoli, "this dish alone would have been enough to establish his reputation." (Imagine a Daniel Boulud or a Mario Batali cementing their reputations on nothing but a broccoli dish today.) Tiberius's son was so crazy about Apician broccoli that the emperor was forced to tell the boy to curb his appetite. The vegetable's popularity was finally expanded about a millenium and a half later when Catherine de Medici moved from Florence to France in 1553 in order to marry the heir to the French throne. Her chefs came with her and introduced broccoli to the country. The Italians are partial to broccoli panfried in olive oil with capers and slivers of prosciutto or maybe a little Parmesan cheese. The French more often take the kinder route with cream and butter in soups or purees.

Brussels sprouts too were once far more popular, and so named because they were considered a Belgian delicacy. Lately they've been enjoying a resurgence, mainly because people have finally learned that the habit of boiling them until they produce a stomach-curdling stench and taste was not, perhaps, the best way to showcase their attributes. Still, for unshakable sprouts haters, the only solution is to disguise them completely by transforming them into a slaw of sorts with the aid of a good knife or food processor. They can then be sautéed in a flavored butter or in bacon fat (and then tossed with crumbled bacon and some fresh thyme). I do this all the time, people love it, and they never know what they're eating. Betty DeCell, my former New Orleans landlady, detests Brussels sprouts, and she fell for it. She also told me about the only other Brussels sprouts dish she ever liked, a puree she had years ago in Austria. I decided to fool around with one and the results were so delicious that it is now my favorite fall accompaniment to roast chicken and veal (and it is especially good with Thanksgiving and Christmas turkeys).

BRUSSELS SPROUTS "SLAW" W
MUSTARD BUTTER

(*Yield: 4 to 6 servings*)

8 tablespoons (1 stick) butter, at room temperature

1 large garlic clove, put through a press

2 to 3 tablespoons Dijon or whole-grain
    Meaux mustard

3 tablespoons minced green onions

2 tablespoons chopped parsley

Salt and freshly ground black pepper

1 pound Brussels sprouts

1 teaspoon caraway seeds or celery seeds, bruised
    in a mortar (optional)

Lemon wedges

Place the butter in a medium bowl and add the garlic,
2 tablespoons of the mustard, the green onions, and the parsley.
Mix well. Add more mustard and salt and pepper to taste and
set aside.

Trim the root ends of the sprouts and remove loose or
discolored leaves. Cut the sprouts in half and then crosswise
into fine shreds. Melt ½ cup of the mustard butter in a large
skillet over medium heat. Sauté the sprouts until tender, about
5 minutes. Lower the heat and stir in the caraway seeds, and

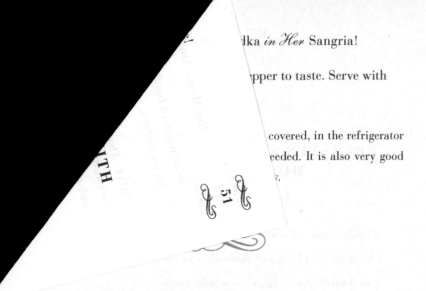

BRUSSELS SPROUTS PUREE

(*Yield: 4 to 6 servings*)

1 pound Brussels sprouts

1 cup heavy cream

3 tablespoons butter

½ teaspoon salt, plus more to taste

¼ teaspoon freshly ground white pepper, plus more to taste

Pinch freshly grated or ground nutmeg

Steam the Brussels sprouts until tender but not soft, about
6 minutes. Set aside.

When the sprouts are just cool enough to handle, slice in
half and pulse in a food processor until finely chopped.

Heat the cream until almost boiling and add to the sprouts
with the butter. Process until smooth. Add 1 teaspoon salt,
¼ teaspoon white pepper, and a pinch of nutmeg, blend well,
and adjust seasonings to taste. Serve warm.

NOTE: For a milder Brussels sprouts flavor, add 1 cup diced, boiled potatoes when processing.

BROCCOLI PUREE WITH GINGER

(Adapted from Cooking with Daniel Boulud*)*

(*Yield: 4 to 6 servings*)

One 2-inch piece ginger, peeled

1½ teaspoons olive oil

1 cup thinly sliced onions

1 large garlic clove, finely chopped

½ cup heavy cream

2 pounds broccoli, trimmed into florets with 1 inch of the stem

Pinch salt, plus more to taste

Pinch cayenne pepper, plus more to taste

Cut off a ¼-inch-thick slice of ginger and reserve. Grate the remainder and wrap it in a thin cotton tea towel. Twist the towel tightly to release the juice. Reserve ½ teaspoon juice and discard the rest with the grated ginger.

Heat the oil in a large saucepan over medium heat. Add the ginger slice, onions, and garlic, cover and sweat until the onions are soft but not browned, 5 to 8 minutes. Add the cream,

bring to a boil and simmer until slightly thickened, about
4 minutes. Discard the ginger slice and keep the cream
warm.

Bring a pot of salted water to a boil. Add the broccoli and
cook until very tender, 8 to 10 minutes. Drain in a colander and
press against the sides with a wooden spoon to extract excess
water.

Put the broccoli in a food processor, add ½ the cream
mixture, a pinch of salt, and a pinch of cayenne. Process until
smooth. Add the remaining cream mixture and the ginger juice;
blend well. Adjust the seasoning and serve warm.

LEE BAILEY'S STEAMED OKRA WITH WARM TOMATO VINAIGRETTE

(*Yield: 6 servings*)

1 pound okra, tips and tops trimmed

4 tablespoons olive oil

4 tablespoons shallots, finely chopped

1 cup tomatoes, peeled, seeded, and chopped (if tomatoes
are not in season, canned are better than the hothouse
varieties)

4 tablespoons red wine vinegar

1 garlic clove, finely chopped

⅔ cup dry white wine

¼ teaspoon salt

Freshly ground pepper to taste

2 tablespoons chopped gherkins

3 tablespoons capers, drained

Stream okra for 5 minutes, or until just fork tender. Allow to cool, but do not refrigerate.

Heat the oil and add the shallots; cook until just wilted. Add tomatoes and simmer for approximately 5 minutes. Add vinegar, garlic, wine, salt, and pepper. Simmer for 15 to 20 minutes, or until reduced to a thick sauce. Correct seasoning. Add gherkins and capers and serve warm over okra.

NOTE: This sauce is also really, really excellent with grilled, steamed, roasted, or simply sautéed fish.

· 6 ·

My Dinners with Jason

Julie had Julia; I had Jason. (Actually, I had Julia, too, but when I made my first quiche from *Mastering the Art of French Cooking* at the tender age of ten, there were no computers, much less blogs.)

I met Jason Epstein in the mid-1980s when I was sent to interview him for *U.S. News & World Report.* He was the legendary editorial director at Random House, a cofounder of both *The New York Review of Books* and the Library of America, inventor of the quality paperback, and editor of Norman Mailer, Vladimir Nabokov, Gore Vidal, and E. L. Doctorow. The subject at hand was the future of the book business, but all I remember of that day was a lively, and lengthy, conversation about food—specifically the importance of brining a loin of pork, a process I'd learned about (long before it became fashionable) in the *Chez Panisse Menu Cookbook,* which Jason happened to have published.

In the more than two decades since, the conversation has continued pretty much uninterrupted: Jason telling me (a

Southerner!) about the excellence of Sherman's memoirs while mixing a perfect martini (vermouth poured into the pitcher and promptly poured out, replaced with Bombay Sapphire gin from the freezer) and serving it with a lemon peel in a thin, thin glass from Harry's Bar in Venice. Jason showing me how to make superior versions of the Chicken Grande from Mosca's outside New Orleans or the lobster roll at Amagansett, New York's Lunch. Jason pressing me into duty to help prepare an outdoor dinner for thirty-five—a gift originally promised by Daniel Boulud in thanks for Jason's publishing his first cookbook (and which he had to apologetically back out of when his then-boss Sirio Maccioni would not let him leave Le Cirque).

He took me to Lutèce before it closed and Daniel as soon as it opened, and invited me into his kitchen while Wolfgang Puck made duck for both of us. Among his first gifts to me were a heavy copper saucepan and a complete set of Edmund Wilson.

That same combination of the literary and the culinary is seamlessly contained in Jason's *Eating: A Memoir.* There's the young Jason in the kitchen of his grandmother Ida, a determined rather than gifted cook to whom he dedicates his recipe for chicken pot pie. There's the teenage Jason making eggs for Gertrude Lawrence in a diner on Cape Cod or enjoying a perfect hamburger beside a lake in Winthrop, Maine. There he is on the *Île-de-France,* honeymooning with his first wife, Barbara, and reading a new translation of *War and Peace.* They ate chicken sandwiches with Chablis for lunch on deck and shared a New Year's Eve table with Buster Keaton, Wilson, and Wilson's then wife, Elena.

Interspersed throughout the charming tales (short stories, really) are wonderful—and wonderfully doable—recipes, written in an equally conversational tone. Though I've rarely seen him follow a recipe himself, he is responsible for some of the great cookbooks—in addition to Boulud, Puck, and Alice Waters, he also published Maida Heatter, Charlie Palmer, and Patrick O'Connell, just to name a few. He met Heatter at Craig Claiborne's annual summer party and by the time he left he'd become her editor. After a single dinner at Chez Panisse, he scribbled the terms of a deal with Waters on a scrap of paper over soufflés and coffee—in part because he wanted the recipe for the "silken fugue" of a bouillabaisse he'd just eaten. The result, two years later, was no less a cultural game-changer than Rachel Carson's *Silent Spring,* which he also published.

Eating is an unpretentious chronicle of an extraordinary life well lived, an antidote of sorts in this age of Rachael Ray and *Iron Chef* and meals made in an ever-decreasing amount of minutes. To read it is to vow to live better, though not necessarily extravagantly. The last recipe in the book is for a simple apple or pear tarte Tatin followed by the words, "And so life goes on." A swell one it is, too, especially when Jason is around to enhance it.

Recently, for example, he e-mailed me his latest variation of a cauliflower puree he's been making in one form or another for years (I've already published a version with curry). It is so easy and so refreshing and as delicious as everything else he's ever shared with me, including the pear tarte Tatin I first tasted on my twenty-eighth birthday, the same one on which he gave me the Wilson book and my now-seasoned—and much treasured—saucepan.

CAULIFLOWER PUREE WITH MINT

(*Yield: 6 servings*)

1 head cauliflower, broken up into florets

1 bunch mint

Whole milk or cream

Butter (optional)

Salt

Freshly ground white pepper

Steam the cauliflower until very tender and put in the bowl of a food processer. Process until pureed, and add mint and ¼ to ½ cup of milk or cream and a tablespoon of butter (this is optional—it makes it a tiny bit richer, but is not necessary for the texture) to smooth it out. Add salt and white pepper to taste.

JASON'S TARTE TATIN

From Eating: A Memoir

Tarte Tatin can also be made with pears (comice are best, just as they begin to ripen). For the traditional tarte Tatin, however, you must use apples, preferably Golden Delicious, which are

*not good eaten raw but hold their shape nicely in a tart.
The tarte Tatin is baked upside down, with the apples under
the crust, which, when the finished tart is flipped, becomes the
bottom. I peel, core, and quarter 4 Golden Delicious apples.
Then, in the copper Tatin pan that I bought from Fred Bridge
fifty years ago, I caramelize a ½ cup or so of granulated sugar
in a ¼ stick of unsalted butter until the sugar becomes the
color of honey. Be careful not to cook the caramel for more
than a few seconds beyond this stage or the sugar will darken
too much. You can move the caramel with a wooden spoon to
even the color, which will be a little darker in some places than
others. Then turn off the flame and wipe the wooden spoon
clean (or the sugar will harden and stick to it).*

*Carefully, for the caramel is burning hot, lay the apple
wedges thick side down in a circle on the caramel, shaping one
of the quarters to fill the center of the circle. Use any remaining scraps to fill gaps and sprinkle a good handful of arrowroot
over the apples to hold the syrup. Now make a crust of simple
pie dough by spinning in a food processor 2 cups of all-purpose
flour with a stick of unsalted butter cut into chunks until the
butter is incorporated but still a little lumpy. Then add a ½
cup or a little less of ice water, a sprinkle at a time, processing
after each addition, until the dough begins to form.*

*As soon as it forms, remove it from the processor onto a
marble slab or plastic sheet, and knead dough into an oblong.
You might enclose the dough in plastic wrap at this point and
let it rest in the refrigerator for a half hour or so to relax the
gluten, or you can skip this step, as I usually do. Then roll out
the dough in a circle about an eighth of an inch thick, place
the tarte pan with its apples (or pears) adjacent to the dough,
roll the dough onto the rolling pin, and place it over the*

apples, discarding the trimmings or saving them for another purpose. With a fork I tuck the edge of the dough down into the pan. Then I slip the pie onto the middle shelf of an oven just under 360 degrees, at which temperature the fruit will not stick to the pan when you turn it right side up. But if you forget and some of the slices stick, just shove them with a wooden spoon from the pan into the gaps where they belong and smooth everything out. When the crust begins to darken, after about 40 minutes, slip the pie out of the oven and let it cool for 10 minutes or so.

Then carefully place the plate on which you plan to serve the tarte over the pastry and flip the pie over. If the syrup is too runny, spoon it back over the pie and with a damp paper towel wipe up any excess syrup from the serving plate. A dedicated tarte Tatin pan is not essential. A well-seasoned iron skillet or even an 8-inch sauté pan will do just as well. Serve the tarte warm with vanilla ice cream.

· 7 ·

Someone's in the Kitchen with Dinah (and Pearl and Ernestine)

When Walker Percy's Love in the Ruins was published in 1971, my father sent a copy to William F. Buckley, Jr., who immediately (and wisely) became obsessed with all things Percy and asked the author to appear on *Firing Line,* his long-running public affairs show. When the deal was done, Daddy flew Buckley in his small plane to see Percy at home in Covington, Louisiana. Percy met them on the little runway, and the first thing he said to Buckley after he disembarked was that he was delighted to meet him, having just seen him a few days earlier on *The Dinah Shore Show.* Though he laughed about it later, Buckley was stunned, and not just a little embarrassed. He'd figured no one whose opinion he actually cared about would ever watch a daytime talk show, and his stint on *Dinah* was not necessarily the first impression he wanted to make on his new hero.

Both men were among the smartest I ever met, but Percy was also a great consumer of pop culture. He took a break from writing every day by tuning into his favorite soap and he once had a passionate conversation with Eudora Welty about *The Incredible Hulk*. One of the few books he ever reviewed was Elmore Leonard's *Bandits*; he was a big fan of Larry King, and, apparently, of Dinah. I thought about them both not long ago when I ran across *Someone's in the Kitchen with Dinah: Dinah Shore's Personal Cookbook* in a used bookstore. The cover features the ageless Dinah herself, all white teeth and perfect blond coif, dishing something out of a pot in a classic 1970s kitchen. When I was a kid, I loved Dinah, too. She had a deep, honeyed voice and was an early cougar—she and the much younger Burt Reynolds were an item for years. What I hadn't known until I came across the title was that she was also a good cook and a prolific entertainer. The book features more than two hundred recipes and anecdotes about guests both on her show and in her kitchen, including one about George Plimpton. (Clearly, Buckley was not her only erudite acquaintance.)

These days, Gwyneth Paltrow gets a lot of ink for being a "real" cook. She did her own PBS show, on cooking in Spain with Mark Bittman and Mario Batali. She wrote a cookbook inspired by her father and she is almost certainly the only actress to have made the cover of both *Vogue* and *Bon Appétit*. She has a niche because none of her contemporaries are fellow cooks. But this was not always the case. Years ago, a friend gave me a copy of *Sophia Loren's Recipes and Memories,* which has a mean Spaghetti al Limone and lots of very glam photos of Sophia in the kitchen and out, with friends like Frank Sinatra, Richard Burton, and Gregory Peck.

My favorite, though, is a treasure called *Pearl's Kitchen: An*

Extraordinary Cookbook by Pearl Bailey. Pearl was another childhood idol—I loved to hear her sing and talk about her husband, the Italian-American jazz drummer Louie Bellson, on *The Tonight Show,* and I remember when Nixon appointed her "Ambassador of Love" to the United Nations. Pearl was born in Virginia and had a ton of soul, and I should have known she'd be a great cook and storyteller. A recipe for Pork Chops and Green Apples, for example, starts off like this: "I had a dinner a few nights ago that was more exciting, actually sexier, than a best-selling novel. What, you may ask, does sex have to do with food? Darlin', I am not going into that right now. Just let me tell you that what got me so excited was pork chops, buttered rice, and Mama's cabbage." A two-page entry on how to make the perfect cup of coffee begins with Pearl's opinion that "women have mind (and men have muscle), but at night . . . the brain sort of turns way down to low," which is why, when she wakes up, "I have to do something to get that baby going again." She reports that when she served Baked Sole Spontaneous "the whole family had a real ball." She rails against aluminum nonstick pans that are way too thin and prefers butter or lard to margarine, which she loathes. There are lots more gems inside, including a recipe for smoked trout by her friend and avid fisherman Bing Crosby and a long riff on how she made her children learn to do housework.

Reading Pearl's book, I thought a lot about my Nashville grandmother's cook, Ernestine Turner—she shared Bailey's imposing stature and larger than life personality and they both cooked a lot of the same stuff like "greasy greens" and fried apples. Ernestine was the president of the Lady Par Busters Golf Club and was forever irritating my grandfather, a member of Augusta National, by winning more and bigger trophies than he did. When I was old enough, I loved going to the Par Buster parties at Ernestine's house. The gin flowed, the food was always fried chicken and potato salad, and Ernestine was always glam. In one of my favorite snaps from those events, she's wearing my grandmother's gold silk dressing gown with frog closures as an evening dress, her arms held high above her head, doing the shimmy.

I spent countless hours in the kitchen with Ernestine and her father, Louis King, who also worked for my grandmother. They taught me how to play poker and to dance the funky chicken, and the first time I ever got drunk, it was on the wine my grandmother let me drink at Ernestine's kitchen-table birthday party. Long after I was old enough to eat lunch in the dining room, I opted to stay at that blue Formica table where the lunches frequently included green beans or black-eyed peas cooked forever with a country ham hock. No matter what was on offer, there was hot water cornbread, a sort of fried cornmeal quenelle I've only ever encountered in middle Tennessee. Deceptively simple, the batter is comprised of nothing but boiling water, cornmeal, and salt, but it has everything to do with the individual cook's hand and intuition. Ernestine's perfect pieces were crispy on the outside, almost silky on the inside, and, when sliced in half and slathered with butter, pretty much the best things anyone ever ate.

When I went off to college she mailed me foil-lined shoe-boxes full of her famous fudge cake and apple cake and when I came back to visit she made the most elegant biscuits and a caramelized leg of lamb for dinner and cheese dreams when my friends came by for drinks. I still can't believe I didn't stand at her side every time she dropped those hot water cornbread "dumplings" into the bubbling grease of her iron skillet or that I didn't beg her to write down more recipes in her flowing hand. I guess I hoped she'd live forever.

Ernestine died of uterine cancer more than twenty years ago and since then I've been trying with mixed success to emulate some of her signatures. The good news is that Pearl does live forever—in print and on the Internet. One of the most joyous YouTube clips I've ever seen is a duet of Pearl and Dinah on a 1960 episode of one of Dinah's early TV shows. Everything, it seems, comes full circle. Like Ernestine and my grandparents, Dinah was from Tennessee, and like Pearl, she was a college graduate. Dinah got a degree in sociology from Vanderbilt in 1938; Pearl earned a degree in theology from Georgetown in 1985. The duet features Dinah singing "Mack the Knife" while Pearl "explains it" and it is impossible to watch without tears in your eyes and an enormous grin on your face—pretty much the same thing that happened whenever I ate Ernestine's cooking.

Below, I'm including recipes for the aptly named "cheese dreams" (easy and decadent cocktail bites) and a warm-weather variation on Ernestine's black-eyed peas. In summer, Ernestine always accompanied the latter with a platter of sliced peeled tomatoes and trimmed whole scallions. Both were such perfect counterpoints to the salty starchy peas that I made a salad of all three ingredients and added fresh basil, an herb that neither Ernestine nor Pearl nor Dinah stuck around long enough to embrace.

While I know I'll never match the sheer crispy/creamy perfection of Ernestine's cornbread, lately I've had help in the form of one of the few recipes I've seen for it in print in *The Gift of Southern Cooking* by Scott Peacock and Edna Lewis. Peacock writes that he'd enjoyed hot water cornbread only in his small hometown of Hartford, Alabama, and that Miss

Lewis, a Virginia native, had never heard of it. Clearly, this stuff is limited to a handful of pockets of the South. In this respect it is similar to another fried bread known as a cala. At the turn of the last century in New Orleans, these rice fritters were such a breakfast staple that "Cala Women" sold them hot from baskets all over the French Quarter. Stephen Stryjewski, chef/co-owner at New Orleans's superb Cochon, substitutes corn in his. They are a bit easier to perfect than the cornbread and would go well with the black-eyed pea salad. When they are on the menu at the restaurant, Stephen serves them as a first course topped with a simple tomato basil salad.

CHEESE DREAMS

(*Yield: About 30 to 40 pieces*)

1 cup (2 sticks) butter, softened

½ pound sharp cheddar cheese, grated

2 tablespoons heavy cream

1 egg

½ teaspoon salt

½ teaspoon dry mustard

1 teaspoon Worcestershire

Cayenne pepper or Tabasco

1 loaf Pepperidge Farm white bread (or a comparable firm white sandwich bread)

Preheat the oven to 375 degrees and lightly butter or oil a cookie sheet.

Cream the butter and cheese in the bowl of an electric mixer. Add cream, egg, salt, mustard, and Worcestershire, and mix well. Add a healthy pinch of cayenne or a couple of shots of Tabasco to taste and blend.

Cut crusts off bread slices, cut into rectangles, and cut in half again. Make a sandwich of two squares by spreading cheese mixture between each piece. Spread cheese on top of each "sandwich" and spread a thin film around all four sides. Place bottom side down on cookie sheet and bake for 15 minutes or until golden brown.

NOTE: These can be assembled either the day before or on the morning of a party and kept on a cookie sheet in the refrigerator. They can also be frozen before baking. Pop them into the oven straight from the freezer; just be sure and allow for a longer baking time.

BLACK-EYED PEA SALAD

(*Yield: 8 servings*)

3 cups fresh black-eyed peas (frozen is fine in a pinch)

1 ham hock or piece of slab bacon

1 teaspoon kosher salt

3 large ripe tomatoes (preferably heirloom), cut in a generous dice, or 1 pint cherry tomatoes, halved

1 small handful of basil leaves, cut in a chiffonade
(you want at least ¼ cup)

1 bunch scallions, sliced, including the pale green part

2 teaspoons cider vinegar

½ cup homemade mayonnaise (see page 85)

Freshly ground black pepper

Place the peas, ham hock or bacon, and ½ teaspoon of the salt in
a medium pot, cover with cold water, and bring to a boil. Simmer
until peas are just tender, which should take anywhere from
25 to 45 minutes—keep checking. Drain peas and set aside.

While peas are cooking, place tomatoes in a large bowl and
sprinkle with remaining ½ teaspoon of salt and let sit for at
least 20 minutes. Do not discard whatever juices the tomatoes
have thrown off. Add peas, basil, scallions, and vinegar and
mix well. Fold in mayonnaise and pepper, and taste to see if
more salt is needed.

To serve, you may add another dollop of mayo on top and
sprinkle with more basil chiffonade, or a sprinkling of the
green parts of the scallions, or both.

NOTE: This will be runny if the tomatoes have thrown off a lot of juice,
but that's what the fried cornbread or the calas are for. The mayonnaise turns pink with the tomato juices and reminds me of the ketchup
my mother used to inexplicably put on top of Ernestine's black-eyed
peas! This is also good with baked cornbread, including Harriet's
Cornbread on page 100. Either way the hot bread is terrific with the
room temp—or cold—pea salad.

HOT WATER CORNBREAD

Adapted from The Gift of Southern Cooking

(*Yield: About 20 pieces*)

1½ cups white cornmeal

¾ teaspoon salt

¾ cup or more boiling water

Cooking oil for frying

Put cornmeal and salt in a mixing bowl and stir to blend. Pour boiling water over and stir until well blended. It should be the consistency of mashed potatoes. If it's too thick, add more boiling water.

Pour about 3 inches of oil in a heavy-bottomed saucepan or deep skillet. Heat oil slowly to 340 degrees. Spoon the batter by rounded tablespoonfuls into the hot oil. Cook for 3 minutes or longer, until golden. They may turn over by themselves; if not, turn once. Drain on paper towels and serve hot with butter.

NOTE: The main thing is to make sure the oil is hot enough, but not too hot. Test fry one piece and slice or break it open. If it's golden brown on the outside but still a little grainy and raw on the inside, the oil is too hot; lower the heat a tad.

STEPHEN'S CORN CALAS

(*Yield: About 10 calas*)

Lard, olive oil, canola, or vegetable oil for sautéing (you
    may also use half butter, half oil—the oil will keep
    the butter from burning)

2 ears fresh corn, cut off cob

1 small onion, diced

1 tablespoon garlic, minced

1 cup cooked white rice

1 bunch green onions, sliced

½ cup flour

2 teaspoons baking powder

1 egg lightly beaten

¾ cup buttermilk

Salt

Freshly ground black pepper

Heat lard or oil in a skillet over medium-low heat, and add
corn, onion, and garlic. Cook until the onion is translucent and
lightly golden. Cool slightly and combine with all remaining
ingredients in a large bowl and mix well.

    In a heavy-bottomed frying or sauté pan (preferably a
well-seasoned cast-iron skillet), heat about 1 ounce of fat and

spoon in about 2 ounces of batter per cake, being careful not
to crowd the skillet. They should look like plump pancakes.
Cook until the edges begin to appear dry, then flip
and cook for another couple of minutes until calas are cooked
through.

· 8 ·

Purple Passion

I once read an essay by historian Bernard Lewis, the West's leading scholar on the Middle East, in which he quoted a fourteenth-century Persian writer on the subject of eggplant: "One day when Sultan Mahmud [who reigned from 998 to 1010] was hungry, they brought him a dish of eggplant. He liked it very much and said, 'Eggplant is an excellent food.' A courtier began to praise the eggplant with great eloquence. When the sultan grew tired of the dish he said, 'Eggplant is a very harmful thing,' whereupon the courtier began to speak in hyperbole of the harmful qualities of eggplant. 'Man alive,' said the sultan, 'have you not just now uttered the praises of eggplant?' 'Yes,' said the courtier, 'but I am your courtier and not the eggplant's courtier.'"

I come to you as the eggplant's courtier. I love it. I love it in Greek moussaka, Provençal ratatouille, and Italian Parmesan. I love the Creole version stuffed with seafood and the Levantine *baba ghanoush*. According to Alan Davidson's invaluable *Oxford Companion to Food,* eggplant originated in

India and was first mentioned in a fifth-century A.D. Chinese text on agriculture. I am grateful that so many cultures have since embraced it, although it took awhile. The Moors brought it to Spain and the Arabs brought it to Italy, but until about 1500, most Europeans considered it inedible, grew it only as an ornamental plant, and gave it derisive names. One of the many that stuck was eggplant, due to the fact that the varieties first introduced to the continent were purple or white in the shape of eggs.

The late, lamented Russian Tea Room paid homage to eggplant's roots in a delicious appetizer called Eggplant Orientale, a not-all-that-Asian cold dish comprised of cooked eggplant, onions, tomatoes, capers, and ketchup, but it was delicious on the restaurant's black bread, and one of my favorite things about the place—in addition to the caviar, the Moscow Mules, and the unparalleled people watching, of course. I once saw Mike Nichols lunching in one of the half-circle booths with Carly Simon, and a year later, when I went to see Nichols's film *Working Girl,* Simon was singing the theme song.

At Galatoire's in New Orleans, the eggplant is fried in thick strips and is always served with little bowls of powdered sugar to mask the eggplant's supposed bitterness. The seasoned bread crumbs do that already, but my husband makes an excellent sweet and sour dipping sauce by mixing Tabasco and a little white wine with the powdered sugar until it's creamy. My mother fries her eggplant in crushed Ritz cracker crumbs, which is slightly decadent, but really, really tasty. In Spain, fried eggplant is frequently served as a tapa. There is a particularly good version at La Trucha in Madrid, but my favorite comes from El Churrasco in Córdoba, where it is fried amazingly lightly and served with *salmorejo,* the thick Andalusian tomato soup, as a sauce.

The big question about eggplant has always been to salt or not to salt. Some people insist that it will be too bitter if you don't salt it first to draw out the juices. Most scholars today say that was necessary only with primitive varieties, but there's another good reason to do it. Eggplant soaks up a whole lot of oil and if you salt if first it will break down the cells so that the flesh won't absorb as much when you cook it. If you do choose to salt it first, cut it in slices or cubes according to how you intend to prepare it, lightly salt the pieces, let stand in a colander for thirty minutes, and pat dry before cooking. In two of the following recipes, there are methods already incorporated to rid the eggplant of both its sponginess and its bitterness (if there is any). And in the recipe from Daniel Boulud, the eggplant is roasted whole, so that any bitter juices will drain off while it's cooling.

Boulud's recipe, by the way, can be easily adapted to incorporate other seasonings and is one of the many reasons he is such a genius as a chef. He made it for my friend Jason Epstein and me one impromptu night in Jason's kitchen. It was so simple to prepare and so delicious I couldn't get over it. Instead of the cumin and onion and duxelles below, I sometimes mix the eggplant with a half cup each of chopped fresh coriander, plain yogurt, and toasted pine nuts, along with a couple of cloves of garlic mashed to a paste. But you could try anything: minced ginger and scallions sautéed in sesame oil, for example, along with a dash of soy sauce.

As for the eggplant salad, it's one of my go-to hot-weather menu staples. A few summers back, I think I served it at every dinner party I gave, along with grilled tuna or lamb, and an easy white bean salad whose only ingredients in addition to the beans are chopped sage, crumbled Gorgonzola, and olive oil.

However you decide to prepare your eggplant, be grateful that the Europeans came to their senses, stopped calling it names, and toted it over to the New World with them (though much of it also came via the African slave trade). Thomas Jefferson grew it in his garden at Monticello, and we Americans, still courtiers in some regards, have been growing—and eating—it ever since.

FRIED EGGPLANT WITH SALMOREJO SAUCE

(*Yield: 4 to 6 servings*)

FOR THE EGGPLANT

1 large eggplant (about 1½ pounds)

4 to 5 cups whole milk

¼ teaspoon salt

1 cup fine yellow cornmeal

1 cup all-purpose flour

Vegetable oil for frying

FOR THE SAUCE

Three ½- to ¾-inch-thick slices country bread, crusts removed (about 1½ cups torn into pieces)

1 pound ripe tomatoes, skinned and seeded

1 garlic clove, minced

¾ teaspoon salt, plus more to taste

¼ cup fruity extra-virgin olive oil

1 teaspoon sherry-wine vinegar (preferable) or red-wine
    vinegar

To prepare the eggplant, peel it and slice across into
⅛-inch-wide slices. Combine 4 cups milk and the salt in a large
shallow baking dish and add the eggplant. Add enough of the
remaining milk to cover the eggplant. Let soak at least 30
minutes before cooking. (You can do this several hours ahead
and refrigerate.)

Meanwhile, to make the sauce, soak the bread briefly
in water and squeeze dry. Place the tomatoes, garlic, and
¾ teaspoon salt in the bowl of a food processor and puree. With
the processor running, gradually add the bread, process until
smooth, and drizzle in the olive oil. Add the vinegar and taste
for salt. Transfer to a serving bowl and set aside.

Preheat the oven to 200 degrees. Mix the cornmeal and
flour in a pie plate. Pour the vegetable oil into a skillet to a
depth of 1 inch and heat until the oil quickly browns a cube
of bread. Remove the eggplant from the milk but do not dry.
Quickly coat the slices with the cornmeal and flour, patting to
make sure it adheres well. Slide the slices into the oil and fry
until golden (a few minutes), turning once. Drain on paper
towels and keep warm in the oven while frying the remaining
slices. Serve immediately, accompanied by sauce.

NOTE: The sauce is also very good on its own, served as a chilled soup
and garnished with sieved hard-boiled egg and chopped Serrano ham
sautéed until crisp in a skillet with a bit of olive oil.

DANIEL BOULUD'S EGGPLANT WITH CUMIN

(*Yield: 6 servings*)

2 medium to large eggplants (about 2½ pounds total)

2 tablespoons olive oil

⅓ cup chopped white onions

1 tablespoon minced garlic

2 teaspoons ground cumin

1 cup finely chopped white mushrooms

Salt to taste

Freshly ground black pepper to taste

Preheat the oven to 425 degrees. Pierce the eggplants in several places so they won't explode, place in a greased baking pan, and bake until soft, almost to the point of collapse, 35 to 45 minutes. Cut in half, cool for 15 minutes or so, and drain the juices. Remove the skin, finely chop the flesh, and set aside.

Heat the olive oil in a large skillet over medium heat. Add the onions, garlic, and cumin, and cover and cook for 3 minutes. Add the mushrooms, cover, and cook for 5 minutes. Add the eggplant and salt and pepper to taste. Cook gently for 20 minutes, or until moisture evaporates. Check for seasoning.

GRILLED-EGGPLANT SALAD
WITH FRESH MINT

(*Yield: 4 to 6 servings*)

3 eggplants (about 1 pound each)

2 tablespoons extra-virgin olive oil, plus more for brushing
eggplant slices

Salt and freshly ground black pepper to taste

3 medium white onions, peeled and chopped

One 28-ounce can peeled tomatoes, drained and roughly
chopped

1 cup firmly packed, roughly chopped or torn fresh mint
leaves

2 tablespoons balsamic vinegar

Prepare a very hot charcoal fire, or preheat the broiler.

Heat a pot of salted water to boiling. Meanwhile, cut the top
off each eggplant and a thin slice off the bottom. Peel a wide
strip of skin off two opposite sides of each eggplant. Holding
the eggplant vertically, slice it lengthwise into ⅓-inch-thick
slices, so that each has a thin border of peel.

Plunge the eggplant slices into the boiling water for 2
minutes. Remove, pat dry, and brush lightly with olive oil.
Place directly on the grill (or on an oiled cookie sheet beneath
the broiler) in a single layer. Turn frequently, every 2 minutes

or so, to make sure the slices don't burn. They are done when they are sizzled brown on the outside (they will be crusty in places, but that's what you want) and just tender within. Season both sides with salt and pepper and transfer to a cutting board. Cut into pieces about 1 inch square, place in a large bowl, and set aside.

Heat 2 tablespoons olive oil in a pan over moderately high heat. Add the onions and sauté for 3 minutes, then add the tomatoes. Cook for a few more minutes; season to taste. Stir into eggplant. Add the mint and balsamic vinegar. Mix well.

NOTE: This is also delicious tossed with pasta, along with about 8 minced anchovy fillets and/or some pitted Niçoise olives. Keep the salad cold or at room temperature and toss with hot spaghetti or linguine.

· 9 ·

Burger Heaven

When I was fourteen years old and a few months shy of the age at which you could then get your driver's license in the state of Mississippi, I wrecked my mother's car. I was sober and it was daylight, but when I backed the big old Buick Estate out of a friend's driveway, the front end somehow swung into a tree. Like everyone else in the Mississippi Delta, I'd been driving since the age of eleven and I thought I was a pro. Clearly, I was not. My parents were out of town, so the first thing I tried to do was get the car fixed, an endeavor that was a bit of an overreach. One, it was a weekend; two, I had no money.

So I did what I thought was the next best thing. I got a job, one that I hoped would make me appear so noble I would avoid getting grounded over the unauthorized use and subsequent wreckage of the "wood"-paneled wagon. I went to work behind the counter at our local McDonald's. A school friend who worked there told me that the manager was a "nice guy" who didn't mind hiring girls slightly younger than the age that the federal government wanted them to be. (We will not dwell on his possible motivation—at that moment, I was grateful.)

When my parents arrived home, I was decked out in my navy-and-powder-blue zip-front polyester pantsuit embroidered with a golden arch and then I showed them the car. Unamused by both dent and outfit, they grounded me anyway. Worse, I was forced to use my initial earnings to pay for the repair. I was furious that my ruse hadn't worked. But then a funny thing happened—I started to love working at McDonald's. I loved the camaraderie and the jokes and the hustle. I didn't mind that every time I went into the walk-in cooler I came out with hair that smelled like Big Mac sauce. I didn't mind greeting the customer with a smile and suggesting a hot apple pie at the end of an order like we had been coached a thousand times to do. I didn't even mind covering for Melvin, the alcoholic manager who mixed bourbon into one of the Coke dispensers for his own sipping pleasure, and I still hope I didn't serve one to an unsuspecting toddler or member of A.A.

Once I paid for the car, I was free to buy my own LPs and eight-tracks (this was a long, long time ago) and a whole closet full of clothes (including an incredibly chic brown velvet suit and a pair of Charles Jourdan pumps I wish I still had). By this time I'd finally become a legal driver and drove myself to work, which meant I was also buying gas and the soft packs of Marlboro reds I had stupidly started smoking. After a year, I was ready to move on, which was a good thing, since the owner of the franchise was forced to pay a hefty fine to the feds once it was discovered that his manager was hiring underage employees.

I still occasionally crave a McDonald's burger—Big Mac sauce is to me like Proust's madeleine. It reminds me of high school and my beloved Mustang convertible and the Bonnie Raitt and Jackson Browne songs I listened to on my way to and from manning the counter. It reminds me of the silver-and-turquoise ring and Clarks Treks I wore with my uniform to show off my "cool chick" cred and the satisfaction I got from the simple act of punching a clock on time. I learned a lot of stuff in my own private Hamburger College, not least of which is the importance of keeping it together no matter what it is that you do. I don't ordinarily quote Snoop Dogg, but in this instance he happens to be on the money: "If it's flipping hamburgers at McDonald's, be the best hamburger flipper in the world. Whatever it is you do, you have to master your craft." This also is why I get seriously irritated when I walk into a fast-food enterprise and I am not greeted with a smile. Or worse, no one suggests to me that I add a hot apple pie with my order, ma'am. I don't want one, but I do know the rules and if I can follow them, anyone can.

These days, most of the hamburgers I eat I make myself. And, like the Big Mac, my burgers are all about the sauce—I keep everything else pretty simple. I am not a fan of piled-on, complex fixings—bacon, sautéed mushrooms or onions, avocado, whatever—that are always too plentiful for the bun and too overwhelming for the meat. In this, I am not alone. The brilliant Eric Ripert once told me, "I love a burger you can take in your two hands and taste all the ingredients in one bite without having it spilling out all over you." He is even a fellow fan of McDonald's. "It may sound crazy coming from a French chef," he told me. "But I think they have the right idea when it comes to size and proportion and classic toppings, so I'm inspired by that—I just use better-quality ingredients."

Also, if a sauce is perfectly tailored for a particular burger, you don't need a lot more stuff—some sweet onion and/or a kosher pickle sliced vertically, along with a couple of leaves of Boston lettuce will do just fine. For buns, I go with English muffins brushed with melted butter and lightly toasted in the oven or plain old soft buns that are crisped up in a sauté pan to mimic a diner's flattop. Just heat enough butter to make a thin film in the pan and add the buns cut-side down for a minute or two.

Like Ripert, I use ground chuck with an 85-to-15 ratio of meat to fat for a beef burger, and if I'm cooking it in a skillet, I finish it off with a couple of shots of Worcestershire sauce. For an everyday burger I dress it with the aforementioned fixings and the basic mayo below, mixed with an extra teaspoon or so of Dijon. My late friend and mentor Kenneth Haxton turned me on to topping a burger with kim chee, which I love with nothing but a bit of the basic mayo. If I feel especially deserving, I reward myself with the black truffle burger that the great Jeremiah Tower always has for his Christmas Eve supper. (For four people, he adds three quarters of a chopped two-ounce truffle to two pounds of ground sirloin or chuck, while the remaining truffle is folded into a fourth of a cup of mayonnaise. He puts each cooked burger onto a buttered, toasted English muffin half, tops it with a tablespoon of the mayo and the other half of the muffin, and serves them all up with a fine red wine.)

Another of my favorite chefs, Suzanne Goin of Lucques, A.O.C., and Tavern, all in Los Angeles, makes a delicious pork burger. At Tavern, she serves it with aïoli and sauce romesco and melted Manchego cheese. Again, I prefer a less-sloppy version with plain mayo or my favorite spicy mayo below (when using the latter, the peppers in the burger should be omitted).

But the possibilities are almost endless. The pork burger, for example, would also be good with a chutney mayo (mix a tablespoon or so of Major Grey's Chutney into the basic mayo and zap it for a few seconds in the Cuisinart). For lamb burgers, I augment the basic mayo with a tablespoon of chopped mint, a half teaspoon of grated lemon zest, and pinch of sugar.

Finally, if you are dying for a bacon cheeseburger, you can achieve a less-sloppy version with a sauce as well. Just fry three or four strips of bacon until crisp. Use the resulting grease for half the oil in the mayo recipe, stir in crumbled bacon when you're done, and add a pinch of good paprika if you want a lovely smoky taste. Use it to dress a burger along with a slice of the best sharp cheddar you can find and you're good to go.

As far as accompaniments, I like the burger to be the main event, and I'd always rather treat myself to French fries someone else has made. Instead, I opt for a side of my mother's tangy coleslaw, which is also really yummy with barbecue.

BASIC MAYONNAISE

(*Yield: 1 cup*)

1 large egg yolk, at room temperature

2 to 3 teaspoons lemon juice

1 teaspoon Dijon mustard (I like Maille)

¼ teaspoon salt

¾ cup Wesson oil (you can also use safflower or canola)

In a medium bowl, whisk together the egg yolk, lemon juice, mustard, and salt until smooth. Still whisking, slowly dribble in the oil until mayonnaise gets thick and the oil is easily incorporated. At this point, you can add the rest of the oil in a thin stream instead of drop by drop. If it gets too thick, add a teaspoon of water.

Spicy Mayonnaise

To 1 cup of the basic mayo, add 1½ teaspoons of Sriracha red pepper paste, 1 pressed garlic clove, 2 tablespoons chopped fresh cilantro, and a squeeze of lime.

SUZANNE GOIN'S PORK BURGERS

(*Yield: 6 burgers*)

Olive oil

¾ cup diced shallots

1 teaspoon ground cumin

2 small chiles de árbol, thinly sliced diagonally, or any dried chili

Kosher salt

2 teaspoons fresh thyme leaves (or a pinch of dried thyme)

3 cups ground pork (about 1½ pounds)

½ cup (4 ounces) Mexican chorizo in small pieces

1 cup finely chopped applewood smoked bacon (about ⅓ pound)

¼ cup roughly chopped parsley

Freshly ground black pepper

Cover bottom of a medium sauté pan with a thick slick of oil. Place over medium-low heat, and add shallots. When oil begins to sizzle, add the cumin and chiles. Stir, then season with salt. When shallots become translucent, stir in thyme leaves, and turn off heat.

In a bowl, combine pork, chorizo, and bacon. Add shallot mixture and parsley. Season with salt and pepper. Using your hands, lift and fold ingredients together until blended. Do not overmix.

Cover bottom of a medium sauté pan with a thin layer of oil, and place over medium-high heat. Form meat into patties that will fit buns; do not make them too thick.

Sauté burgers until browned on bottom. Turn them, basting with fat in pan. When browned on both sides, cut a slit in one patty to check doneness; it should be only slightly pink.

JUDY'S SLAW
(*Yield: 6 servings*)

3 tablespoons Wesson oil

¼ cup cider vinegar

1 teaspoon salt

½ teaspoon freshly ground black pepper

½ teaspoon Colman's dry mustard

1 teaspoon celery seed

2 tablespoons sugar

3 cups chopped cabbage

¼ cup finely chopped green pepper

½ teaspoon grated white onion

Whisk oil and vinegar together in a large bowl. Add salt, pepper, mustard, celery seed, and sugar and whisk until blended.

Chop cabbage, either by hand or in a food processor (if you use the food processor, do it in three batches to ensure it chops evenly). I like mine pretty finely chopped, but you can chop it in pieces up to a half-inch square. Fold cabbage into dressing. Fold in onion and green pepper and check for seasonings.

· 10 ·

Summer on a Plate

I am in England as I type this, out in the coun-tryside near Northampton at my friend Alexander Chancellor's stunning Inigo Jones house, where, between fleeting moments of sunshine, it is gray and cold and generally pouring down rain. But it is also the day before summer officially begins and I am about to make a salad. In fact, we've been rather determinedly making salads at every meal for the last three days now—running out to the garden with head down and hood up to grab a handful of rocket (arugula) and snip a few herbs. These we've tossed with endive and little gem lettuces, olive oil from Tuscany, a squeeze of lemon, and a judicious pinch of Maldon sea salt. It may not feel like summer outside, but inside we have summer on a plate.

The Brits have long gotten a bum rap about their cuisine. These days, of course, there are brilliant chefs cooking all over London, but people who should know better persist in thinking of English food as mostly bangers and mash, bubble and squeak, lots of overboiled potatoes, and great haunches of meat. It turns out, though, that what they've always been very big on are salads.

My friend and former *Vogue* colleague Vicki Woods, whose own English garden is overflowing with rocket and mint, and basil and chives (not to mention masses of gorgeous English roses), turned me on to Robert May's *The Accomplisht Cook*. May, one of England's first professional cooks, published his recipe for Another Grand Sallet in 1660, but it sounds almost exactly like what I've been doing for the last few days: "All sorts of good herbs, and little leaves of red sage, the smallest leaves of sorrel, and the leaves of parsley pickt very small, the youngest and smallest leaves of spinach, some leaves of salad burnet, the smallest leaves of lettuce, white endive and charvel, all finely pickt and washed and swung in a strainer of a clean napkin and well drained from water: then dish it out in a clean scowered dish . . . with good oil and vinegar."

Three hundred years later, the great English food writer Elizabeth David wrote, "It seems to me that a salad and its dressing are things we should take more or less for granted at a meal, like bread and salt." Her seminal *A Book of Mediterranean Food* reintroduced her war-deprived countrymen to the pleasures of olive oil and herbs, as well as such exotica as gazpacho and "a salad of aubergines."

Now, fifty years on, we have Nigel Slater, the food columnist for the *Observer*, whose book, *Tender*, is a beautifully illustrated chronicle of the bounty from his London garden. There are all sorts of wonderful recipes—Vicki swears by the celery gratin, which elevates that humble garnish to a grand main event—but you can tell that salad is Slater's number one love. "If there was a recipe that stood for everything I believe about good eating," he writes, "it would be the quiet understatement that is a single variety of salad leaf in a simple bowl. Each leaf should be perfect, the dressing light and barely present, the whole effect one of generous simplicity."

As they say over here, good point, well made. Below, you will find his recipe for A Lemon Dressing for Summer. I also include a lovely cucumber salad from David's *Summer Cooking* that I've tinkered with ever so slightly to allow for the almost toxic quality of most grocery store tarragon vinegars. Like May's seventeenth-century recipe, both are written plainly in the way that people actually talk.

Slater's recipe is pretty much the same thing I make most nights, and is similar to one that Deborah Madison, the great vegetarian chef, uses to dress a fennel, mushroom, and Parmesan salad, that has long been a favorite. The trick with the mushrooms is to marinate them for a bit in some of the vinaigrette—I've never been able to fathom why anyone would add raw mushrooms, which have the taste and texture of Styrofoam, to a salad when it is so easy to infuse them with flavor first. Elizabeth David knew that, of course—in *Summer Cooking,* she includes a mushroom salad that couldn't be simpler. First, she says, put a half pound of sliced white mushrooms in a bowl. Next, "squeeze lemon juice over them, stir in a little chopped garlic, season with ground black pepper, and pour a good deal of olive oil over them. Immediately before serving salt them and add more olive oil, as you will find they have absorbed the first. Sprinkle with parsley, or, if you have it, basil, or a mixture or fresh marjoram and lemon thyme." I can attest that the latter combination is especially delicious.

NIGEL SLATER'S A LEMON
DRESSING FOR SUMMER

(*Yield: 1 cup*)

Mix together a pinch of salt, a teaspoon of Dijon mustard, and
the juice of half a lemon. Beat in a scant cup of olive oil and a
teaspoon of grated lemon zest. Leave for a few minutes for the
ingredients to get to know one another.

ELIZABETH DAVID'S "CUCUMBER
AND CHIVE SALAD"

Adapted from Summer Cooking

(*Yield: 4 servings*)

A cucumber, a few chives, a few tarragon leaves, and, for the
dressing a ½ cup of cream, a teaspoonful of sugar, olive oil, salt
and pepper, a teaspoonful of sherry wine vinegar.

Peel the cucumber and slice it paper thin. Sprinkle coarse
salt over the cucumber and leave it in a colander to drain for
half an hour.

Mix the sugar and vinegar together, then add the cream, pepper, and salt. Add about 2 tablespoons of olive oil and the chopped chives and tarragon, and pour the dressing over the cucumber in a shallow dish.

NOTE: One of my very favorite outdoor suppers consists of this salad with a simple roast chicken and the best premier cru Chablis I can afford. You really don't need much else, though some warm crusty bread and salty butter wouldn't be bad and neither would some roasted mushrooms—just add a pound of trimmed white mushrooms to the roasting pan with the chicken about 30 minutes before it's done and roll them around in the pan juices with a little salt. For a completely perfect evening, finish off with something cold and lemony like the lemon soufflé on page 204.

DEBORAH MADISON'S FENNEL, MUSHROOM, AND PARMESAN SALAD

(*Yield: 4 to 6 servings*)

1 garlic clove

¼ teaspoon coarse sea salt or kosher salt

2 to 2½ tablespoons lemon juice

2 strips of lemon peel, minced

⅛ teaspoon of fennel seeds, crushed under a spoon or in a
    mortar

4 to 5 tablespoons extra-virgin olive oil

8 ounces large, firm white mushrooms, wiped clean

Freshly ground black pepper

1 fennel bulb

1 tablespoon fennel greens, chopped

1 tablespoon Italian parsley, coarsely chopped

Salt

3 ounces Parmigiano-Reggiano, shaved into paper-thin slices

Pound the garlic and the salt in a mortar until smooth. Stir in lemon juice, lemon peel, fennel seeds, and olive oil.

Thinly slice the mushrooms. Dress them with a few tablespoons of the vinaigrette, and season them with plenty of pepper. Lay a piece of plastic wrap directly over them to keep them from browning and set aside for about an hour to marinate.

Trim the fennel bulb and cut into quarters. Remove most of the core, then slice it lengthwise, very thinly, leaving the pieces joined together. Dress it with most of the remaining vinaigrette and half the herbs, and season with salt and pepper. Add the rest of the herbs to the mushrooms.

Layer the mushrooms, cheese, and fennel on each plate and spoon the remaining vinaigrette over the top.

NOTE: This salad does not have to be composed. I've made extra dressing and done it as a tossed salad using a handful of whole parsley leaves or a combo of parsley leaves and romaine leaves, either torn up or sliced about an inch wide. You still need to marinate the mushrooms, but then you can just throw everything else in a bowl with the parsley and lettuce and toss. Made like that, a bit of extra cheese doesn't hurt.

· 11 ·

The Tyranny of
Summer Produce

Every summer I make at least one or two visits to my parents' house in Mississippi, and I don't think I've ever departed without the following image in my rearview mirror: my mother running down our gravel driveway, slightly wild-eyed, and carrying an armload of corn, which she is screaming at me to take. "Wait, wait, you *have* to take these, please take them with you, *please*."

Now, I am crazy about corn but by the end of every trip, I'll have already consumed a ton of the stuff in almost every possible incarnation, including corn pudding, corn fritters, corn "fried" in butter or bacon grease, and, of course, corn on the cob, either grilled or steamed or zapped in its husks in the microwave (a procedure that not only instantly steams the corn, but makes it easier to remove the silks). But every summer I stop, and every summer she fills up my backseat with countless ears.

Welcome to the Tyranny of Summer Produce. Depending on where you are, by August or early September late-summer corn abounds, squash and zucchini are falling off the vine, birds are after the figs, tomatoes and blueberries are bursting, peaches and plums shriveling. Then there are the herbs: parsley and dill are going to seed; basil and tarragon and mint are becoming impossibly leggy. The pressure to keep up with it all is just too much—and so is the guilt. There's almost a moral obligation to consume such wondrous bounty, but Mother Nature moves a lot faster than we do. "You can't even feed the hungry," says Bobby Harling, the playwright and screenwriter (*Steel Magnolias*; *Soapdish*) who is also a great cook. "You could try, but you'd have to do it in two days."

Bobby reports that at this time of year in his hometown of Natchitoches, Louisiana, the church parking lot after Sunday services is in a constant state of "vegetable gridlock," while amateur gardeners like his father try to pawn off bushels of okra and corn and peaches on friends not equally burdened. Professional farmers have the same sense of urgency—or, perhaps, disgust. "It gets to the point where the folks selling the tomatoes at the farmers market are like, 'Just take them—we don't even want any money,'" says my friend Stephen Stryjewski. One summer he took so many he ended up making ten gallons of ketchup he had no idea what to do with.

I'm not actually complaining. I love Stephen's salad of shaved summer squash with mint and goat cheese, for example, and my mother's kitchen is always an excellent place to be—especially when her kitchen counter is crowded with late summer Arkansas Traveler tomatoes, which she peels and slices at every meal. Most nights during this period of vegetable tyranny, we don't even bother with meat. Mama will make her corn succotash with baby butter beans, or I'll make mine with okra and tomatoes. She'll make her sublime fried eggplant or an eggplant casserole with tomatoes and shrimp; I'll make my eggplant salad. We are both big on casseroles that utilize at least two overabundant vegetables, thereby emptying out twice the fridge space—I was ecstatic a few years ago when I discovered Craig Claiborne's cheesy gratin of both corn and zucchini.

I'm even more ecstatic when our neighbor Mary Lou Sandefur, who cultivates an entire field of basil each summer, turns up at the door with jars of her homemade pesto. We toss it in pasta, of course, but it also it perks up slow-roasted plum tomatoes and sautéed summer squash with onions (the yellow and green together is gorgeous). I add some to the food processor with butter beans to make a great spread for toasted slices of baguette, and my friend M. T. smashes it with fingerling potatoes that she's boiled or roasted to excellent effect.

But back to the corn. The pesto is delicious slathered on grilled corn on the cob, too—there are few herbs, in fact, that don't go well with corn. I sauté it in butter with mint and chives, and in olive oil with chopped jalapeño and cilantro. A long-ago Hamptons houseguest turned me on to a dish comprised of half steamed rice and half corn, mixed together with a ton of butter and chopped parsley. In her book *Sunday Suppers at Lucques,* Suzanne Goin includes a delicious sauté of corn and thin-sliced cabbage with green onion, thyme, and bacon that she tops with seared salmon, and she combines corn, brown butter, and sage as a starting-off point for lots of pasta sauces (Try tossing the latter with lump crab and fettuccine, but it's delicious on its own.)

It should be noted that even though it's likely that corn will be included in an end-of-summer supper, cornbread should not be ignored. Nor should dessert, which is a great way to use up all those peaches that always fill up the space on my mother's counter not already crowded with tomatoes. When another generous neighbor stops by with zinnias from his own big field, pretty much the whole meal, including the centerpiece, can be summed up with the now ubiquitous phrase "farm to table." Most folks who grew up like I did have always known that it's a practical and utterly delicious way to eat—even if the farm is sometimes a bit too overwhelming for the table.

MY SUCCOTASH

(*Yield: 6 to 8 servings*)

6 strips bacon

1 medium yellow (or, preferably, Vidalia) onion, minced

1 jalapeño pepper, seeded and minced

3 cups sliced okra

4 ripe tomatoes, diced

4 garlic cloves, minced

1 teaspoon salt

¼ teaspoon freshly ground black pepper

2 teaspoons chopped fresh thyme leaves

6 ears of corn, shucked and scraped

Cayenne pepper

8 fresh basil leaves, torn into pieces

Cook the bacon slices in a large heavy-bottomed skillet or sauté pan until crisp. Leaving the rendered bacon fat, transfer bacon to paper towels to drain.

Add the onion and jalapeño to the drippings, and cook, stirring occasionally, over low to medium-low heat until vegetables begin to soften, about 4 or 5 minutes. Turn the heat to medium, add the okra and sauté for 5 minutes, stirring frequently. Add the tomatoes, garlic, salt, black pepper, and thyme. Turn heat down to medium-low. Cook for another 3 or 4 minutes, then add the corn kernels (and any accumulated milk), and simmer until corn is tender, about 10 minutes, stirring occasionally, making sure to scrape the bottom.

Stir in a dash of cayenne pepper and the basil leaves. Crumble reserved bacon and sprinkle on top.

NOTE: Stir in some raw peeled large Gulf shrimp during the last 5 minutes or until they are just cooked through; you'll have a great main course.

MARY LOU'S PESTO

(*Yield: About 4 cups*)

4 cups basil leaves, removed from stem

1½ cups freshly grated Parmesan cheese

1 cup walnuts or pine nuts

4 large garlic cloves

1¼ cups extra virgin olive oil

½ to 1 teaspoon salt

½ to 1 teaspoon freshly ground pepper

Rinse basil leaves and dry thoroughly. Place them in the bowl
of a food processor with the cheese, nuts, and garlic, and pulse
until mixture is ground to a paste. Add oil slowly, until texture
is creamy. Add salt and pepper to taste and mix well.

HARRIET'S CORNBREAD

(*Yield: 8 servings*)

Butter for greasing pan

1 small can cream-style corn (8 ¾ ounces)

½ cup Wesson oil

1 cup sour cream

1 cup white cornmeal

1½ teaspoons baking powder

½ teaspoon salt

2 eggs

Preheat the oven to 350 degrees. Generously butter a number 5
iron skillet or a corresponding heavy ceramic or glass casserole
dish.

Put all ingredients in a bowl and mix well. Transfer to a blender or food processor and process for a minute, or less, until mixture is smooth and liquefied.

Pour into prepared pan and bake for 45 minutes.

STEPHEN STRYJEWSKI'S SQUASH AND ZUCCHINI SALAD WITH GOAT CHEESE AND SPICY PECAN VINAIGRETTE

(*Yield: 4 to 6 servings*)

FOR THE VINAIGRETTE

1 cup pecans

2 tablespoons butter, melted

1 teaspoon salt

½ cup olive oil

¼ cup sage leaves, cut into a chiffonade

1½ tablespoons finely chopped garlic

1 tablespoon seedless chili flakes

⅓ cup sherry vinegar

Freshly ground black pepper

FOR THE SALAD

1¾ pounds yellow squash, cleaned, trimmed, and sliced very thinly, lengthwise (a mandoline is helpful here or a good vegetable peeler)

1¾ pounds zucchini, prepared as above

½ sweet onion, sliced very thinly

1 cup arugula leaves

½ cup packed mint leaves

½ cup packed parsley leaves

4 ounces goat cheese, crumbled

Salt and freshly ground black pepper

Preheat the oven to 325 degrees. Toss pecans with melted butter and the salt. Spread on a baking sheet and toast for about 20 minutes, shaking the pan to redistribute about midway through, until golden brown. Cool and crush roughly with a rolling pin. Blend the remaining ingredients.

Toss salad ingredients with ½ cup of the vinaigrette, season with salt and pepper.

DRINKING

· 12 ·

Of Pimm's and Paris

*More than twenty years ago, I canceled a wed-*ding to a man who I still very much cared about. So, in a seriously misguided attempt to soothe the would-be groom's feelings—and much to the disbelief of my mother and many other equally sane people—I agreed not to cancel our French honeymoon. I thought I was doing the civilized thing. I thought I'd be letting him down easy, that he could save face with friends and family (many of whom lived in Paris) if he could say it was the wedding and not necessarily the marriage I was afraid of. There also was the fact that we already had first-class tickets, a suite at L'Hôtel, and, on my end, a particularly swell trousseau.

We got over the first hump, the bottle of champagne left in the room to welcome the new "Mr. and Mrs.," by drinking it—very quickly. My jilted groom spent his days catching up with fellow foreign correspondents; I spent mine with my then colleague at *Vogue,* André Leon Talley, and George Malkemus, CEO of Manolo Blahnik U.S.A., who happened to be in town. André himself had a new wardrobe for the wedding, including a white piqué suit with a fuchsia silk lining and a double-breasted seersucker suit with matching shoes made up by Manolo. Dressed to the nines, we lunched at Caviar Kaspia or on the Ritz terrace. We shopped at Madeleine Castaing and an ancient place George knew where I bought ropes of green cut-glass beads that looked like emeralds.

I wore the latter with a white silk dress to dinner à deux with my former intended at Jamin, Joël Robuchon's first restaurant in Paris. Tucking into Robuchon's justifiably famous potato puree (accompanied by lots of Château Giscours, which was my ex's favorite), I remembered why I'd fallen in love in the first place. But the next morning we were off to Lyon, a city not nearly so romantic or containing a single soul we knew, and by the end of day two we'd almost killed each other. (I think we actually might have killed the Michelin three-starred chef Alain Chapel—all the electricity went off in his restaurant the night we dined there, and he died of a stroke less than forty-eight hours later). By that point, I'd begun to feel as though a piano wire was being stretched through me, so I called André, who instructed me to get myself immediately on the fast train back to Paris where he would meet me at the bar at the Ritz.

Like all of André's advice, it was excellent, not least because it led to my discovery of the Pimm's Royale. I had already imbibed plenty of Pimm's Cups at the Napoleon House in New Orleans, where it is an improbable specialty, and I'd attended a garden party or two in the British countryside, where they are summer fixtures. But what I'd enjoyed in those venues were classic Pimm's Cups, made with Pimm's No. 1 and a refreshing topper of fizzy "lemonade" (usually

7UP) with a cucumber garnish. Pimm's, by the way, was invented in the 1840s by James Pimm, a London oyster bar owner who blended gin with quinine and a secret mixture of herbs. The Pimm's Cup is a wonderful summer refresher, but the Pimm's Royale is one of the world's great drinks.

At the Ritz, where I arrived before André, it came in a short-stemmed goblet much like a brandy snifter, accompanied by the usual slice of cucumber, but also a sprig of mint, lots of sliced fruit, and a seriously potent brandied cherry. The main difference though, was that the lemonade was replaced by very good Brut champagne. After the first one, I felt better than I had in weeks. The brandied cherry in the second made my blood rush almost as fast as the train I'd just disembarked. When the third one came, I vowed to call it quits, but then André arrived and there seemed no point in stopping, so we sipped and held court well into the night with fellow Ritz drinkers including the actress Arlene Dahl (to whom I poured out my story) and a group of former Los Angeles Rams who were serving as Madonna's bodyguards during her European tour. By the time my almost-groom turned up with his sister, I was really happy to see them, and the evening remains one of the most entertaining and memorable of my life.

The bill, not surprisingly, was also memorable, but in the end it was a small price to pay for finishing the "honeymoon" off in style and maybe even with some modicum of grace. I kept it as a reminder that even misguided intentions sometimes end up being not so crazy and that Paris can be a forgiving place—Humphrey Bogart and Ingrid Bergman are not the only ones who will always have it, after all.

Since then, the Pimm's Cup's popularity has spread far beyond Parisian bars and English lawns. I serve it in one in-

carnation or another at all my warm-weather gatherings—
the Aussie chef Pete Evans's version includes homemade
sparkling lemonade and looks especially pretty in a glass
pitcher for crowds. The drink also has been taken up by many
bartenders who add their own touches by doing everything
from muddling the cucumber with lime (very nice) to incor-
porating all manner of liqueurs and flavored syrups. Chris
Hannah, the drinks maestro at another New Orleans institution, Arnaud's French 75 Bar, adds watermelon syrup to surprisingly good effect.

PIMM'S ROYALE

(*Yield: 1 drink*)

1¼ to 1¾ ounces Pimm's No. 1

Brut champagne

Cucumber slice

Apple slice (optional)

Lemon slice

Orange slice

Mint sprig

Brandied cherry (optional)

Pour Pimm's over ice cubes in a large wine goblet or highball
glass. Top with champagne and add garnishes.

PETE EVANS'S PIMM'S CUP

(*Yield: 4 to 6 drinks*)

8 ounces Pimm's No. 1

4 ounces lemon juice

2½ ounces simple syrup

1 cucumber sliced

1 orange sliced

¼ cantaloupe chopped

4 to 6 mint sprigs

¼ cup grapes

2 cups club soda

Add all ingredients to a carafe with some ice and stir well.

CHRIS HANNAH'S PIMM'S CUP
WITH WATERMELON

(*Yield: 1 drink*)

1 medium-size watermelon

1 cup sugar

2 ounces Pimm's No. 1

1 ounce lemon juice

2 ounces ginger ale or 7UP

Sliced cucumber, berries of any type, and mint sprig for
garnish

Puree and strain enough watermelon to make one cup of juice.
In a small pan, heat the sugar and watermelon juice and boil
until the sugar dissolves. Remove from heat (mixture keeps in
the refrigerator for weeks.)

In a cocktail shaker with ice, add Pimm's, lemon juice, and
1 ounce of the watermelon syrup, and shake. Strain into an
ice-filled Collins glass. Top with ginger ale or 7UP and garnish
generously with cucumber, berries, and mint.

NOTE: The watermelon syrup is a fine thing indeed to keep in your
fridge and is a great addition to mojitos, margaritas, and any number
of vodka drinks.

· 13 ·

Gin!

To those among us who define their seasons by the cocktails they consume, the spring and summer months almost invariably come under the heading of "G&T weather." Now a lot of the people who persist in using this phrase tend to wear smug expressions and Guccis with no socks, and are not, therefore, included in the ranks of folks whom I consider ideal drinking partners. Still, the fact remains that the gin and tonic is a drink that almost begs to be consumed as temperatures rise, and we would all do well to pause and consider its merits.

First, the gin. Gin is a highly distilled grain-based spirit flavored most strongly with juniper berries, but also with a wide array of botanicals that, depending on the distiller's recipe, can range from coriander, cardamom, and almonds to dried lemon and Seville orange rinds. The wildly popular and relatively new Hendrick's Gin contains hints of rose petals and cucumber; the Philly-based Bluecoat is made in small batches with organic botanicals and triple filtered water, and, like Hendrick's, is relatively new (introduced in 2006 as opposed to, say, Gordon's, which first appeared in 1769). One of my literary heroes, John D. MacDonald's "salvage expert" Travis McGee, drank Plymouth and sometimes Boodles. People who do this kind of stuff for a living report that Plymouth starts off with hints of citrus, coriander, and caraway seed, and finishes with a mild juniper flush. Boodles, on the other hand, starts sweet, finishes dry, and contains whiffs of everything from citrus and mint to nutmeg and rosemary.

In its infancy, gin was not nearly so complex and certainly not as subtle. Made by a Dutch professor of medicine, it was named "Essence of Genièvre" (the French word for juniper) and promoted as a diuretic. After the Dutch Protestant William of Orange assumed the British throne, it became enormously popular in England, not least because William imposed punitive tariffs on imports from the Catholic winemaking countries and promoted the local distillation of *jenever,* which his subjects shortened to "gin." As the empire expanded, so did gin consumption—even in the North American colonies the Quakers were known for their custom of imbibing gin after funerals.

The gin and tonic is said to have been invented as a way for the Englishmen in tropical colonies to get their daily dose of quinine, a derivative of the bark of the cinchona tree and, for three hundred years, the only effective cure for malaria. (The required citrus wedge had the added benefit of fighting scurvy.) Winston Churchill, a devoted gin fan (he mostly drank Plymouth), once said, "The gin and tonic has saved more Englishmen's lives, and minds, than all the doctors in the Empire." The "minds," I'll buy. But the effective treatment of malaria requires as many as three 350 milligram doses of quinine per day, while 6 ounces of tonic water contains less than 20 milligrams. By that math, only the heroic Churchill himself could take both the medicine and the gin and remain standing.

Which leads us to the tonic. These days most of the widely available commercial stuff is so wimpy and so heavily sweetened with corn syrup it's a wonder it wasn't outlawed by New York City mayor Michael Bloomberg. Your best bet is to search out either the Fever-Tree or the Q Tonic brand or to make your own (easily done, courtesy of mixologist Brooks Reitz's Jack Rudy syrup and some club soda). The first time I tasted a G&T with house-made tonic (and Plymouth gin), it was at New Orleans's aptly named Bar Tonique. It was also a revelation—after one bracing swallow, I understood completely why all those Brits were content to stick around India and perpetuate Her Majesty's Empire.

It may not cure malaria, but even a little quinine is surely better than none, and one can never be too careful. In New Orleans, for example, mosquitoes are extremely plentiful and epidemics of malaria are not an altogether distant memory. So it is that I look forward to the seasonal switch, like many others before me. A character in Padgett Powell's lovely *Edisto Revisited,* for example, was partial to the summertime combination of gin and tonics with country ham. Ernest Hemingway was partial to pretty much all things alcoholic but in *Islands in the Stream,* he has his alter ego, Tom, expound on the virtues of a gin and tonic in a way that only an obsessive drinker can. When the barkeep Bobby asks, "Do you really like the taste of that stuff?" Tom says, "I like the quinine taste with the lime peel. I think it sort of opens up the pores of the stomach or something. I get more of a kick out of it than any other gin drink."

By all accounts the Queen Mother got a kick out of gin and tonics all year round, and, encouragingly, she lived to be 101. (There's a possibly apocryphal story in which she yells out to two of her gossiping retainers: "When you old queens have finished, this old queen would like a gin and tonic.") When Doris Lessing became the second-oldest Nobel Prize winner for literature, the *London Times* reported that she celebrated with a G&T, and that was in October. Most of the rest of us partake primarily in the summer, when many other refreshing gin cocktails are also frequently on offer. Among the most popular is the Tom Collins, made with gin, lemon juice, and simple syrup and topped with club soda. When FDR's cousin entertained the visiting Churchill by serving him one, he promptly spat it out. I imagine it was the sugar—she would have fared better, perhaps, with a Gin Rickey, made with gin, lime juice, and club soda. My father insists that he build his first business by bombing around the Mississippi Delta armed with a thermos full of Gin Rickeys on the floorboard of his Buick. In the ninety-eight-degree summer heat, an icy Rickey greatly eased his ability to sell grain bins to farmers. He and his business partner once tried mightily to finish a story that began "Remember that time we were up on the combine in Holly Bluff?" I never heard the end of it because they started laughing so uncontrollably that they threw napkins over their faces and wept for long minutes. Apparently there were Gin Rickeys involved.

The Rickey was invented in a Washington, D.C., bar called Shoemaker's in 1883 by a "gentleman gambler" named Colonel Joe Rickey, who was not in fact a colonel but a lobbyist. Washington is by far the most unbearable of all the unbearably hot places I've ever lived, so it's not surprising that the "colonel" needed a refresher. There is less certainty about the origins of a Southside (essentially a Tom Collins with mint), a drink more at home in a private club on Long Island, one of the places where it is said to have originated, than in a D.C. saloon or the soybean fields of the Mississippi Delta. Depending on who's telling it, the Southside was an invention of: the Southside Sportsmen's Club, where moneyed New Yorkers repaired to hunt, fish, and enjoy the powerful gin drink on offer at the bar; Prohibition-era Chicago's notorious Southside gangs who were forced to mask their inferior hooch with sugar, mint, and citrus; or the '21' Club, which began life as Jack and Charley's speakeasy and where it has long been a signature drink. I have no special insight, but my money is on '21,' not only because I love the place, but because theirs is a particularly excellent Southside, whose punch is unimpeded by the soda that's usually added.

In New Orleans, two more recent gin refreshers have entered the fray, the delicious sage julep at John Harris's Bouligny Tavern and a Straddling Thorsten, a drink of my own invention. Many more years will have to pass before I can reveal the full story behind its name—suffice it to say it involves a Nobel Prize winner, a lusty blonde in a white leather miniskirt, and a group of Chinese brain scientists, and you can take it from there. Based on the now-shuttered La Caravelle's Alberto No. 1, it is much like a Southside with lime instead of lemon and has a champagne topper that encourages a certain lightness of spirit. As it combines two of Churchill's very favorite elixirs, gin (it's especially good with Hendrick's) and champagne (Churchill only drank Pol Roger), I bet he would have swallowed it.

GIN RICKEY

(*Yield: 1 drink*)

½ ounce fresh lime juice

2 ounces gin

Club soda

Pour or squeeze the lime juice into a Collins glass filled with ice. Add the gin, top with club soda, and stir.

THE '21' CLUB SOUTHSIDE COCKTAIL

(*Yield: 1 drink*)

2 ounces vodka

Juice of 1 lemon

2 teaspoons extra-fine sugar

1 tablespoon fresh mint leaves

Place all ingredients in a shaker and shake vigorously to bruise mint leaves. Strain into chilled Collins glass filled with ice.

NOTE: To make a Southside Fizz, use at least one more teaspoon of sugar and top with club soda.

BOULIGNY TAVERN'S SAGE JULEP

(*Yield: 1 drink*)

3 sage leaves
½ ounce simple syrup
½ ounce lemon juice
1½ ounces Aviation Gin
Crushed ice

In a mixing glass, muddle sage with simple syrup lightly to extract oils. Add lemon juice and gin. Fill a Collins glass with crushed ice. Pour liquid over crushed ice, leaving muddled leaves on top of ice.

THE STRADDLING THORSTEN

(*Yield: 1 drink*)

Juice of 1 lime

2 teaspoons powdered sugar

10 whole mint leaves

2 ounces gin

Champagne

In a shaker, combine lime juice and powdered sugar. Stir until dissolved. Add mint leaves and muddle with spoon. Add gin and ice; shake and pour into stemmed wineglass. Top with champagne and garnish with a mint sprig.

NOTE: You can also pour this over ice in a brandy snifter or oversized wineglass.

· 14 ·

Men and Martinis

Plenty of notable women have been crazy about martinis. In the film *Every Day's a Holiday,* the ever-reliable Mae West urged Charles Butterworth to get out of "those wet clothes and into a dry martini." Dorothy Parker wrote a much-quoted poem about three martinis putting her under the table and four putting her "under the host." *Will & Grace*'s inimitable Karen Walker once asked for a martini "and don't waste any space with those olives," while a slightly more earnest M. F. K. Fisher wrote that "a well-made dry martini or Gibson, correctly chilled and nicely served, has been more often my true friend than any two-legged creature."

Like Parker, Ogden Nash came up with an amusing verse about martinis ("A tingle remarkably pleasant . . . I wish that I had one at present"), as did Cole Porter ("They've learned that the fountain of youth/ Is a mixture of gin and vermouth"). Robert Benchley, Parker's fellow Algonquin wit, had plenty to say on the subject (and uttered a variation of West's line in the film *The Major and the Minor* five years later). H. L. Mencken called the martini "the only American invention as perfect as a sonnet."

But the thing about men and martinis is not what they say but how they look—few things make a man appear more elegant than having one in hand. A case in point is the marvelous Slim Aarons photograph of Clark Gable, Van Heflin, Gary Cooper, and Jimmy Stewart leaning against the bar at Romanoff's on New Year's Eve 1957. They are all in white tie, they are all cracking up, and they all exude a level of masculinity and cool that is breathtaking. Gary Cooper is holding what looks like a straight-up martini. It may well have been champagne, but I prefer to think not.

Romanoff's, the Rodeo Drive restaurant that closed in 1962, was enormously popular among the stars of the day, as was Chasen's, another Los Angeles landmark that closed in 1995. Chasen's was famous for its chili (Liz Taylor had several quarts flown to the set of *Cleopatra*) and a martini called Pepe's Flame of Love. Created by Chasen's bartender Pepe Ruiz, the latter was made with Stolichnaya vodka, sherry instead of vermouth, and orange peel—flamed over the glass with some fanfare—rather than lemon. Legend has it that Dean Martin, another very cool cat, complained that he was bored with regular martinis and the dramatic new drink was the response. Before Chasen's closed in 1995, I enjoyed many of Pepe's Flames, along with that old-fashioned (flaming) masterpiece Steak Diane, made tableside, and I can attest that both were excellent.

These days, some of the finest martinis in the world are made in the bars of London hotels—usually by Italian bartenders. I am partial to the bar at Duke's, where bar manager Alessandro Palazzi starts with a frozen glass and garnishes the finished product with either the peel of an Amalfi lemon or olives from Puglia. James Bond creator Ian Fleming is said to have written part of *Casino Royale* at Duke's, a location that obviously inspired him. The novel (Fleming's first Bond book) is the one in which Bond creates the Vesper, the martini he names after the gorgeous double agent Vesper Lynd. According to Bond's instructions to the casino barman, the Vesper should be served "in a deep champagne goblet" (which means that my man Cooper could well have been drinking one), and made with "three measures of Gordon's, one of vodka, half a measure of Kina Lillet." It should then be shaken "very well until it's ice-cold" and garnished with a "large thin slice of lemon peel." The result was enough to impress Bond's CIA contact Felix Leiter: "Gosh, that's certainly a drink."

Like Bond, my father is partial to Gordon's, mainly because it has less alcohol than most other gins, enabling him to drink more of it. When I was in grade school he taught me to make his martini a little on the wet side and garnished with an onion, which technically makes it a Gibson, and paid me ten cents per drink. For Christmas one year, I collected my earnings and bought him a sterling silver vermouth dropper, which I am fairly certain he never used. He still drinks martinis though, and he is still partial to fellow martini drinkers. During one of his many trips to Washington, he spied Bill Blass in the Jockey Club bar with a straight-up martini happily in hand. After ordering one of his own, he introduced himself and they became fast friends. On the face of it, they were an unlikely pair: a world-famous dress designer and a businessman/politico from the Mississippi Delta. But Blass exuded the same sort of masculinity and cool as Gary Cooper, and Clarke Reed could easily have held his own with that bunch at Romanoff's. All of them knew how to "hold" their gin, in every sense of the word.

Blass died before the rise of the Cosmopolitan, the Lemon Drop, the Appletini, and, worst of all, the Chocolatini. But I'm sure he'd agree that serving something in a martini glass does not a martini—or indeed a perfect sonnet—make. I'm an anomaly among most of my female friends for standing firmly against the Cosmo in particular, but there is one "feminine" martini I do endorse, the Ginger Martini from Birmingham's Hot and Hot Fish Club, which substitutes Cointreau for vermouth and adds a bit of ginger syrup. Someone once paid tribute to the martini's elegance by calling it "Fred Astaire in a glass"; I think I'll privately rename Hot and Hot's cocktail the Ginger Rogers in tribute to Astaire's dance partner.

While I drink plenty of them, I also sort of agree with Lowell Edmunds, author of *The Silver Bullet: The Martini in American Civilization,* that vodka martinis should be classed with "polyester fabrics, supermarket tomatoes, and books printed on toilet paper as a symptom of anomie." Put another way, my friend Jay McInerney, a self-described martini "constructionist," says, "I like my martinis with gin, so that they taste like something, and enough vermouth to add complexity—otherwise it's just gin and not a cocktail at all, and where's the genius in that? I'm an olive man, although lately I have fallen under the spell of Hendrick's gin with a slice of cucumber. That's as innovative as I get." He adds that he prefers them shaken and straight up, "of course."

I'm with Jay and 007—I love those tiny shards of ice floating at the top of a straight-up martini that can only come from vigorous shaking. But there is a strong contingent in favor of stirring. Supposedly, shaking a martini dissolves too much air into the mix—the "bruising" of the gin that some martini drinkers complain about. Somerset Maugham said stirring was the superior method "so that the molecules lie sensuously one on top of the other." Clearly, Maugham was a man who had given his martinis a lot of passionate study.

The only other serious point of debate is the garnish. Mixologist Brooks Reitz, bar manager of Charleston's Fig Restaurant, sometimes substitutes a silver-dollar-sized piece of grapefruit peel for the traditional lemon, which is actually sort of nice. At Galatoire's in New Orleans, the waiters hedge their bets by bringing what I call a "martini salad" to the table, a small bowl of lemon peel, cocktail onions, large green olives stuffed with pimientos, and green olives stuffed with anchovies. After two or three martinis, it's pretty much all you need for dinner.

Just in case, I include a recipe for Steak Diane, below.

PEPE'S FLAME OF LOVE

(*Yield: 1 drink*)

½ teaspoon fino sherry, chilled

Three 2-inch orange peels

2¼ ounces chilled vodka, preferably Stolichnaya, chilled

Chill a martini or cocktail glass thoroughly. Add the sherry to the glass and swirl to coat completely, pouring out any excess.

Take one of the orange peels, light a match, and squeeze the orange peel sharply, so that the oil is propelled through the flame and onto the inside of the glass. Repeat so that the oil evenly coats the glass, and discard the peels.

Shake or stir the vodka with ice to chill, and strain into the coated glass. Squeeze the remaining peel over the drink and around the rim of the glass and drop it into the drink for garnish.

NOTE: When the practiced Chasen's bartenders flamed the orange peel, it would usually briefly ignite the sherry in the glass to very good effect. But you don't have to be a showman to make the drink—it's all about the perfect combination of flavors, and the orange oil releases nicely even without a flame.

THE VESPER

(*Yield: 1 drink*)

3 ounces gin

1 ounce vodka

½ ounce Lillet Blanc

Long thin peel of lemon

Place gin, vodka, and Lillet in a cocktail shaker with ice. Shake vigorously and strain into deep champagne *coupe* or cocktail glass. Twist or bend the lemon peel, rub around the edge of the glass, and drop it into the drink.

THE HOT AND HOT FISH CLUB GINGER MARTINI

(*Yield: 1 drink*)

4 ounces Tanqueray Rangpur or other lime-infused gin

1 ounce Cointreau

¾ ounce ginger simple syrup

1 ounce apricot brandy

1 piece candied ginger

Chill a martini glass at least 20 minutes before serving. Place the first 4 ingredients in a shaker filled halfway with ice. Shake until well chilled. Strain into the glass and drop the candied ginger into the bottom.

NOTE: To make the ginger syrup, combine 1 cup sugar and 1 cup water in a saucepan. Add about ¼ cup of peeled and julienned ginger and bring the mixture to a boil. Cover, remove pan from heat, and let the ginger steep for 30 minutes. Strain through a fine mesh strainer and refrigerate.

STEAK DIANE

(*Yield: 4 servings*)

4 steaks, weighing about ½ pound each and cut about
   ½ inch thick from a tenderloin or boneless sirloin

Freshly ground black pepper

Salt

Olive or peanut oil

5 tablespoons butter

¼ cup finely chopped shallots

¼ cup finely chopped parsley

¼ cup cognac or brandy

¼ cup slightly reduced veal or beef stock or beef bouillon

1 tablespoon Dijon mustard

2 teaspoons Worcestershire sauce

Juice of ½ lemon

A few drops Tabasco sauce

Trim the meat of any fat, and pound each steak between two
sheets of wax paper until they are almost ¼ inch thick. Season
each side of steaks with a couple of grinds of pepper and
sprinkle with salt.

Heat oil in large skillet or sauté pan over medium-high heat
and add 2 tablespoons of the butter. Just as the butter begins to

brown, add steaks, two at a time. Cook for 40 seconds on the first side, 30 seconds on the second side, and remove to warm platter. Repeat with other two steaks. (Steaks should barely color and will become just springy to the touch.)

Add remaining 3 tablespoons of butter to skillet and when foaming, stir in shallots and parsley. Let cook for a minute, then, tilting pan away from you, add cognac and flame. When flame has burned out, add stock, mustard, Worcestershire sauce, lemon juice, and Tabasco. Stir or whisk to combine and simmer for a minute. Turn off heat, place steaks back in pan to bathe in sauce, remove to platter, and pour remaining sauce over them.

· 15 ·

The Importance of
Holiday Cheer

More than once, when writing about the holi-
days, I have quoted the ever-reliable Oscar Wilde: "After a
good dinner, one can forgive anybody, even one's relatives."
There is no question that the food is important. The odd
chopped black truffle or two studding the mashed potatoes,
say, or even a really good squash casserole, can go a long way
toward repairing frayed nerves. Conversely, an overcooked rib
roast or the wrong kind of pie can be the potentially dangerous
last straw. One year, my grandmother's Christmas rolls were so
hard that my grandfather threw one down the table at her,
sending it splashing into the gravy boat. Since then, I've learned
to hedge my bets with Sister Schubert's fail-safe frozen yeast
rolls, along with copious amounts of festive refreshment, a
strategy I'm sure Wilde would have enthusiastically supported.

The point is that after enough punch, people tend not to
care, or even notice, that the rolls haven't risen, that little broth-

er's girlfriend has a nose ring (or five), that some of the people assembled haven't actually spoken a civil word to each other in more than forty years. This is pretty much the theme of singer-songwriter Robert Earl Keen's infectious and spot-on anthem, "Merry Christmas from the Family," which starts out with the line, "Mom got drunk and Dad got drunk at our Christmas party." Of course they did. The song is populated by ex-wives and new wives, irritating cousins and Mexican boyfriends, and other members of the extended clan that most of us try to avoid until the holidays inevitably roll around and we are forced together in the name of some misguided family unity.

Keen's crowd makes the best of the proceedings by drinking champagne punch, homemade eggnog, margaritas, and Bloody Marys ("'Cause we all want one!"). In between, there are numerous trips to the Stop 'N Go and the Quickpak Store for everything from Salem Lights and a can of fake snow to a bag of lemons and some celery for the aforementioned Bloodies. While I, too, am an errand-running fool during the holidays (what better way to appear useful while also getting the hell out of the increasingly fraught house), I am not so ambitious with regard to the drinks. Punch or eggnog, followed by the best wine you can afford, should do it. For one thing, an elegant silver punch bowl puts the sheen of propriety on the fact that what you're really doing is serving up a big batch of holiday denial.

Made the old-fashioned way, punch is also, to quote one of my father's highest compliments, "strong stuff." When he uses the term, it's usually in reference to a good-looking woman or an especially funny anecdote, but I'm sure its derivation comes straight from the punch bowl. Cocktail historian David Wondrich explains that punch was the forebear of the cocktail, originating in sixteenth-century England, where it consisted of fairly rough wine "drowned" with sugar and lemon and spices, and augmented with stronger spirits and lots more citrus once the Brits made it to India and beyond. No matter where it ended up, Wondrich says the punch of the seventeenth thorough nineteenth centuries bears as much relation to the anemic stuff served at today's teas and banquets as "gladiatorial combat does to a sorority pillow fight."

Consider, for example, the Junior League of Savannah's cookbook's recipe for Chatham Artillery Punch, which calls for a gallon of gin, a gallon of rye, a gallon of cognac, 2 gallons of rum, 2 gallons of Catawba wine, and 12 quarts of champagne. The punch, long a point of Savannah pride, was the house brew of the city's all-volunteer regiment, founded in 1786 and described by Wondrich as "a social register militia that spent far more time parading and partying than it did loading cannons and shooting them." Which might have been just as well. In 1883, a Georgia journalist wrote that "we are living witnesses to the fact that . . . when it attacketh a man, it layeth him low and he knoweth not whence he cometh or whither he goeth." One way to get rid of one's peskier relatives, I suppose, is simply to kill them with the stuff. Or you could give them a couple of cups and watch them kill each other. When Wondrich whipped up a batch for a recent food and wine festival in Atlanta, he warned the participants, "I have seen bad things happen from drinking this."

Savannah is not the only Southern city whose punch recipe can be put to good holiday use. Charleston's militia had a punch too, the Charleston Light Artillery punch, a delicious version of which, containing brandy, peach brandy, and Jamaican rum, is served at Sean Brock's irresistible Husk.

Then there's Charleston's St. Cecilia Society Punch, a classic brandy, rum, tea, champagne mixture that's always served at the annual ball of the august society, formed in 1763 and named for the patron saint of music. In 1896, the *Baltimore Sun* reported that there is "no social organization in America so old or so exclusive" and that the balls are "characterized by dignity." Maybe so, but after the only one I ever attended (a boarding school running mate was being presented), I woke up with my date on a park bench in an evening gown and missed two subsequent airplanes out of town. As a result, I prefer the slightly more refined punch recipe given to me by my friend Laura Steiner from Montgomery, Alabama, where it is something of an institution. First published in the cookbook of the local Episcopal Church ladies, it consists mainly of champagne, Sauternes, and brandy, and is especially pretty with a decorated ice ring.

But then even the stoutest punches can be things of beauty. My hero Charles H. Baker, Jr., the professional bon vivant, intrepid world traveler, and occasional drinking buddy of Ernest Hemingway, gets borderline teary-eyed over the "Ritual of the Punch Bowl" in the *Exotic Drinking Book* volume of his seminal *The Gentleman's Companion*: "Few things in life are more kind to man's eye than the sight of a gracefully conceived punch bowl on a table proudly surrounded by gleaming cohorts of cups made of crystal or white metals, enmeshing every beam of light, and tossing it back into a thousand shattered spectra to remind us of the willing cheer within."

Baker's book contains an extensive section on punch, but there's mention of eggnog too, specifically one considered a "Scottish institution" (who knew?) from the Clan MacGregor, "a lovely, forceful thing based on brandy, Bacardi, and fine old sherry." I was never a huge fan of eggnog, from Scotland or anywhere else, preferring the milk punches that are ubiquitous in New Orleans, where I live. But that was before I tasted the version made by my friend Mimi Bowen, who grew up in Memphis and who now owns a very chic New Orleans boutique that bears her name. The recipe comes from Mimi's grandmother and namesake Myrium Dinkins Robinson via her aunt, Lynn Robinson Williams, whom Mimi calls the "Auntie Mame of Memphis." Aunt Lynn, who died in her bed on her ninety-sixth birthday with both a cigarette and a glass of champagne in hand, sounds like someone with whom I would've actually enjoyed spending the holidays. Well into her eighties, when she finally passed the recipe along to Mimi, she put it in the mail with a note reading, "For your file. Don't lose it." I reprint it below exactly as she typed it.

WORLD'S GREATEST EGGNOG

  4 cups bourbon
  2¼ cups sugar
  12 large egg yolks
  8 cups whipping cream

Pour bourbon into large mixing bowl. Stir in sugar and let sit several hours. Overnight, if you can wait. Beat egg yolks until they are an ugly yellow color. Fold them into the bourbon and sugar mixture. Let sit for 2 hours if you can wait. Whip the cream until very stiff, fold into the bourbon and egg mixture. Let sit for 1 hour if you can wait. Mixture may be cut in half if you are clever enough to know how to divide 2¼ by two! Serve in cups. Serves 20-30 people. Nutmeg not permitted! ENJOY.

MONTGOMERY CHAMPAGNE PUNCH

(*Yield: About 24 servings*)

1½ cups sugar

2 cups lemon juice

1 cup brandy

2 bottles champagne, chilled

1 bottle Sauternes, chilled

Combine sugar and lemon juice, stir until lemon is dissolved, and chill.

Just before serving, mix this combination with brandy and pour over an ice ring in a large punch bowl. Gently stir in champagne and Sauternes. Float orange and lemon slices in the bowl.

FOR THE ICE RING

Procure a ring mold (as for tomato aspic) or an angel food or bundt cake pan that will fit into your punch bowl. Scatter

orange and lemon slices evenly on the bottom of the pan and
sprinkle with brandied cherries. Fill the pan with ice cubes to
hold fruit in place and then pour in cold water to the top.
Freeze for a few hours or overnight. Remove from freezer just
before serving. Briefly hold the pan upside down in the sink
beneath a stream of hot water to separate ice from mold.

· 16 ·

One Two Punch

Several years ago, when Quentin Tarantino made Elmore Leonard's *Rum Punch* into a film called *Jackie Brown,* it captured almost none of the book's genius. Leonard's work is deceptively multi-layered, full of mood and pitch-perfect rhythm. The action is entirely unforced; plot twists that come out of nowhere are somehow altogether believable. Most important, there's never been an Elmore Leonard novel that contains a single thing it shouldn't.

The latter, especially, could not be said of the appalling mixtures that often constitute an actual rum punch, which, when crafted as meticulously as the work of my hero, can offer the same restorative—if slightly off-kilter—faith in the generally entertaining reliability of even the darkest sides of human nature. Too often, people make like Tarantino and show off by trying out not-quite-successful retro references (think ceramic pineapples or paper umbrellas) or adding such heavy-handed ingredients as frozen limeade and cranberry juice cocktail.

In her book *Rum Drinks,* the culinary historian Jessica

Harris reminds us that rum punch is as old as rum itself. A strong, unrefined quaff, rum was perfect "for a world that required a little muting around the edges," she writes, specifically the brutal culture of the sugarcane growing, slave-trading islands of the Caribbean in the sixteenth and seventeenth centuries. During this period, the per capita intake of Barbados reached a whopping 10 gallons, much of it (by the ruling classes, at least) in the form of Planter's Punch, of which there were as many versions as there were plantations. That early rum had a viscous texture that needed at least as much muting as the environment in which it was imbibed. Individual planters offset the oiliness by mixing rum with cane syrup, a touch of island spice (usually clove or nutmeg), and the juice of whatever citrus they happened to grow.

In the 1860s, a Cuban named Facundo Bacardi figured out how to refine rum, producing a smooth beverage that could blend well with a wide range of mixers that were used to enhance, not mask, the taste of the liquor. Thus, the daiquiri, including Hemingway's favorite, the Papa Doble (a double shot of white rum shaken with both grapefruit and lime juices and a bit of maraschino liqueur) was born. It also meant that unlike any other liquor, rum almost begs to be mixed with itself. Mixologist Dale DeGroff, aka "King Cocktail," once explained to me that despite the fact that there are literally dozens of different styles of rum, the molasses base is so consistent you can mix dark and light, spicy with not spicy, aged and young, high proof and low, all to good effect. DeGroff says that most good rum punches call for at least two rums, and sometimes a third as a floater on top. "You'd never think about mixing three Scotches or two gins," he says. "It would be disgusting."

Alas, a lot of what has been done to rum in recent times, especially in my adopted home of New Orleans, is also pretty disgusting. Drive-through daiquiri shops sell sickly sweet frozen daiquiris flavored to mimic everything from a White Russian to a margarita. When made properly, Pat O'Brien's great contribution to rum punches, the Hurricane, is delicious; in most places on Bourbon Street, it is transformed into a powerful, but particularly vile version of hot pink Hi-C.

It doesn't have to be this way. DeGroff, who was famous for his Planter's Punch when he presided over Manhattan's Rainbow Room, finds it the most "elegant" of rum punches, but designates the mai tai as the "most sophisticated and interesting." Ever the willing student, I decided to test them both— and many more—on a recent sojourn to my mother's beach house. My good friend and Florida neighbor Joyce Wilson, who lived in Hawaii for years, contributed the recipe for the mai tai. She'd procured it from Honolulu's Halekulani Hotel, where they serve at least a hundred of them a night, and it was as advertised—complex and packing a delicious punch in the form of a 151-proof floater.

Elizabeth Cordes, a seasoned mix-mistress, contributed the Peach Daiquiri. Now, I love a classic daiquiri like the many I enjoyed years ago at Havana's Floridita (or, indeed, like the excellent Haitian daiquiri at New Orleans's Herbsaint). But in a pinch, both Elizabeth and I have been known to pull into a daiquiri drive-through. We knew we could improve on anything those establishments have to offer—plus, we had a plethora of farm stand peaches on hand. Also, since we were running low on white rum, we decided to apply the rum punch rule of adding at least two different rums to great effect.

Finally, the three of us experimented with the one that started it all, the Planter's Punch. DeGroff, who gives his version a rosy glow with the addition of grenadine, turns out to be justifiably renowned for his creation. But another, seemingly off-the-beaten-path version also caught our collective eye, courtesy of Charles H. Baker, Jr., the world-class imbiber and author of four invaluable volumes known as *The Gentleman's Companion* and *The South American Gentleman's Companion*. Called a Savannah Planter's Punch, Baker's discovery combines rum and brandy, a partnership that actually makes a lot of sense. After all, French brandy was the slave trade's primary means of exchange until rum replaced it in the late eighteenth century. Further, Savannah was often a West Indian colonial's first mainland step before reaching England.

Which leads us back to my man Elmore. Like his work, rum's history is packed with vivid examples of man's many transgressions toward his fellow man. In addition to the fact that rum fueled the trans-Atlantic slave trade for more than three hundred years, a pirate gave his name to Captain Morgan rum, and Churchill once dismissed British naval traditions as "rum, sodomy, and the lash." There's not a lot we can do to make up for that, but we can offer up at least a modicum of redemption in the form of a carefully made cocktail that shows rum the respect it finally deserves.

HALEKULANI MAI TAI

(*Yield: 1 drink*)

MAI TAI MIX:

½ ounce orgeat syrup

½ ounce orange curaçao

½ ounce simple syrup

¾ ounce Bacardi Gold rum

¾ ounce Bacardi Select rum

1¼ ounces lemon juice

½ ounce Lemon Heart 151 rum

Combine mai tai mix ingredients and pour over crushed ice. Add Bacardi rums and lemon juice. Gently pour Lemon Heart rum on top so it floats.

The Halekulani bartenders are instructed to garnish each drink with a lime wedge, a lime wheel, a sugarcane stick, a mint leaf, and a Vanda orchid. You could easily get by with only the lime and the mint.

NOTE: If you don't have a good jigger, mixing is made easier when you remember that ½ ounce is the equivalent of 1 tablespoon.

FROZEN PEACH DAIQUIRI

(*Yield: About 4 drinks*)

8 to 10 ripe peaches, peeled and cut into chunks

4 ounces white rum

4 ounces Mount Gay rum

¼ cup fresh squeezed lime juice

¼ cup simple syrup

Ice

Myers's rum

Fee Brothers peach bitters

Put the first five ingredients in a blender. Turn the machine on for a minute or two until the ingredients are blended, and then add ice until you reach the desired consistency. (Ours was slushy, not frozen hard and smooth like those from a drinks machine. We liked it a tad loose, with the odd chunk of peach.)

Test for sweetness, as you may have to add more simple syrup or lime, depending on the sweetness of your peaches. If desired, float a little Myers's on top—we loved the way the dark rum played off the peach flavor. And to really gild the lily, get hold of a bottle of Fee Brothers sublime peach bitters and add a few drops to the Myers's after floating it on top.

DALE DEGROFF'S PLANTER'S PUNCH

(*Yield: 1 liter or about 6 drinks*)

5 ounces dark rum (Dale likes Myers's)

5 ounces white rum (Dale likes Appleton White)

3 ounces orange curaçao

6 ounces fresh orange juice

6 ounces pineapple juice

3 ounces simple syrup (one part sugar, one part water)

½ ounce St. Elizabeth Allspice Dram Liqueur

3 ounces fresh lime juice

3 ounces grenadine

1 tablespoon Angostura bitters

Pineapple, orange, and lime slices, for garnish

Mix all the ingredients together in a large pitcher or punch bowl. Before serving, shake the drinks individually in a cocktail shaker with ice and strain into a large goblet or punch cup filled three-quarters of the way with ice. Garnish each drink with pineapple, orange, and lime slices.

SAVANNAH PLANTER'S PUNCH
(*Yield: 1 drink*)

2 ounces Jamaican rum (like Myers's or Appleton Estate
    Dark)

3 ounces cognac

Juice of 1 lime

¾ ounce fresh pineapple juice

Pineapple, cherries, and orange slice, for garnish

Mix all liquids together in a shaker or pitcher. Pack a crystal
highball glass or silver julep cup tightly with finely shaved ice.
Pour in the pre-mixed liquids, stir briskly for a moment with
a long spoon or swizzle stick. Garnish with a finger of ripe
pineapple, a cherry, and an orange slice. Serve when the glass
frosts.

· 17 ·

Champagne Charlotte

On my nineteenth or twentieth birthday, I can't remember which, I announced that from that moment on I would drink nothing but champagne. Never mind that I was still in college and living with two other girls in an apartment on the first floor of a Georgetown townhouse. Never mind that my disposable income at that point consisted of the roughly fifty dollars a week I made working in *Newsweek*'s Washington bureau and the largesse of my roommate Nora Cooney, whose father, Ace, had—incredibly—given her one of the first gold American Express cards I'd ever seen. Never mind that it was illegal for me to drink anything alcoholic whatsoever.

In retrospect, my birthday declaration was not just laughably pretentious but also ill-advised—providing, as it did, further evidence of my penchant for what used to be called "high living" that still makes my father crazy. I should take this opportunity to remind him that it was he who first took me to places like the Jockey Club when I was all of fourteen and he who introduced me to the Georgetown hostess Susan

Mary Alsop. (It should be noted, too, that Susan Mary's ex-husband, the columnist Joe Alsop, once referred to his brother John and my father as "Champagne Charlies," when they dropped him at an important dinner and made their own way out on the town.) I was included in so many of both Susan Mary's and Joe's august gatherings as the token "young thing" that my mother was forced to allow me the use of her own Neiman Marcus card to buy a proper evening wardrobe. I had, therefore, drunk a lot of champagne (if memory serves, Susan Mary was especially partial to Bollinger), and I liked it. A lot. Also, I'd seen that quote from Madame de Pompadour about champagne being the "only wine that leaves a woman beautiful after drinking it." And then there was John Maynard Keynes, who said his only regret at the end of an otherwise productive and celebrated life was not having drunk more of the stuff. I figured I'd get a move on.

I'm pretty sure that within the month I was back to drinking beer and Scotch and everything else I still drink, but I've never lost my deep love for those golden bubbles. I remember my first sip of Cristal (in a Paris hotel room with a future fiancé and my friend McGee who'd made a well-timed delivery of the Clairol electric rollers I'd asked to borrow), and my first sip of Krug (in Paris again, at Karl Lagerfeld's *hôtel particulier*, where Elton John also played the piano—it was a very good night). But what I never fell for was a champagne cocktail. Maybe it was the Angostura bitters that define the original recipe and which are still not among my favorites. Maybe it was an aversion to screwing around with something already pretty perfect—and not just a little expensive. Whatever it was, I've since come around—hard. As usual, it was a McGee that did it. In this case, McGee's sister Elizabeth.

It was my first Thanksgiving in New Orleans and I was spending the day with Elizabeth's two girls and her late husband. Mike was an excellent but slightly obsessive cook who'd spent two whole days on the chocolate cake that would end the meal. I knew better than to bring anything that would mess with his long-planned menu. But I also knew Elizabeth adored champagne cocktails and I'd just received a galley of what would be Simone Beck's last cookbook. So I whipped up a batch of very un-Thanksgiving-like tapenade to nibble on while Mike cooked, and made the base for Simca's Champagne Cocktail, along with some macerated cherries for its garnish.

Elizabeth and I toasted the day with two or three cocktails, and then Mike joined us and we drank some more (one bottle of champagne, by the way, will make six drinks). By the time we sat down at the table, I remember thinking that it might be the best Thanksgiving I'd ever had. I know it was the longest—we didn't eat the cake until the next morning and Elizabeth and I stayed up chatting until well into the night. In 1937, Billy Wilder made a movie called *Champagne Waltz* and its tagline was "As gay and sparkling as a champagne cocktail!" Naturally, we were, too.

Since then I've come to love a French 75 (with gin, the way it was first made in 1915 at Paris's New York Bar), a Black Velvet (created in 1861 at Brooks's Club to mourn the passing of Prince Albert), and a Death in the Afternoon, a potent concoction invented by Ernest Hemingway for a 1935 celebrity bartender's guide. I have even come to love bitters, especially the vast array available from Fee Brothers, a fourth-generation family-owned company in Rochester, New York. At Bar Tonique, an excellent and very chic establishment on Rampart Street in New Orleans, I was turned on to a particularly refreshing champagne cocktail containing a sugar cube doused with Fee Brothers' grapefruit bitters rather than the usual Angostura. I have since become the drink's chief proselytizer and the trio—champagne, the bitters, a box of La Perruche cubes—is now my go-to host or hostess gift, for which I am always profusely thanked.

The first published recipe for the Champagne Cocktail appeared in "Professor" Jerry Thomas's seminal work, *How to Mix Drinks, or The Bon-Vivant's Companion*, published in 1862. (The song "Champagne Charlie" became a hit six years later.) Thomas's ingredients were "one-half teaspoonful of sugar, one or two dashes of bitters, and one piece of lemon peel," and his instructions were to "fill tumbler one-third full of broken ice, and fill balance with wine." His readers were also told to "shake well and serve," but before the century was out, people figured out that a cube of sugar saturated with bitters at the bottom of a glass would dissolve slowly and evenly, so that both the shaking that hastened the champagne's flatness and the ice that watered it down could be avoided.

Thomas's original formula remains very much in vogue, but almost immediately there were variations. In the 1920s, a barman at London's Savoy Hotel began serving one that added equal parts Grand Marnier and cognac to the bitters-soaked cube and garnished it with an orange twist rather than lemon. And then of course there were offshoots, including the great French 75. So named because the combination of gin and champagne delivered a kick not unlike the one supplied by the powerful French 75mm field gun of World War I, the drink was popularized at war's end at New York's Stork Club. Early on, rival recipes substituted cognac for the champagne and a current version, known as a French 76, substitutes vodka.

Either way, it is delicious. It also "hits with remarkable precision," the warning included by author Harry Craddock in his *The Savoy Cocktail Book,* published in 1930. Duly noted.

FRENCH 75

(*Yield: 1 drink*)

1 ounce gin

½ ounce fresh lemon juice

½ ounce simple syrup

Lemon twist

Pour the gin, lemon juice, and simple syrup into a shaker with ice and shake vigorously. Strain into champagne flute and fill to top with champagne. Garnish with twist.

NOTE: One of the many wonderful variations on this drink calls for adding a ½ ounce of Cointreau. Substitute an orange twist for lemon.

RITZ 75

(*Yield: 1 drink*)

1 ounce fresh lemon juice

1 ounce freshly squeezed mandarin orange juice

½ ounce simple syrup

1 ounce gin

Champagne

Lime slice

Orange slice

Cherry

Mix the lemon juice, orange juice, and simple syrup in a tumbler. Add lots of ice. Pour in the gin and top with champagne. Garnish with citrus slices and a cherry.

NOTE: While I love the elegance of champagne cocktails made in flutes, there is nothing more refreshing than a citrusy champagne "highball." This variation of a French 75, created at the Paris Ritz, is a perfect example. In summer, I add mint to the garnish.

SIMCA'S CHAMPAGNE COCKTAIL

(*Yield: 6 drinks*)

⅓ cup sugar

½ orange, sliced

¼ lemon, sliced

½ cup cherries, macerated in brandy

¼ cup brandy or cognac

1 bottle champagne

Mix the first five ingredients in a jar and refrigerate for at least 1 hour or overnight. Strain.

Place a macerated cherry in bottom of champagne glass. Add about an ounce of the chilled mixture and fill with cold champagne.

BLACK VELVET

(*Yield: 1 drink*)

Guinness

Champagne

Fill a champagne flute halfway with Guinness. Carefully and slowly top with champagne.

NOTE: For a Brown Velvet, substitute Bass Ale for the Guinness.

DEATH IN THE AFTERNOON

(*Yield: 1 drink*)

1 ounce Pernod or absinthe

Champagne

Pour absinthe into a flute and top with chilled champagne.

NOTE: There will be a pleasant cloudy effect to this cocktail.

· 18 ·

The Yucca Flats

The summers of my youth were spent largely at the house of our neighbors the Yarbroughs, who had six children (including three good-looking, much older, and very funny boys) and a "playroom" outfitted with a pool table, a card table, a stereo, and an ancient refrigerator. Depending on the summer, I was invariably in love with one of the brothers or their friends, and it was in their company that I picked up the skills that have contributed to my good health and happiness ever since: how to kiss, play poker (mostly penny-ante bourre and five-card draw), hold my beer, and hum along to pretty much every song on a nonstop vinyl soundtrack that included—but was not limited to—the Allman Brothers, the Rolling Stones, the Yardbirds, and the Sir Douglas Quintet.

The most memorable summer was marked by the introduction of the Yucca Flats—not the nuke site, but a passioninducing concoction mixed in a galvanized metal garbage can with floating handfuls of squeezed citrus—and I've always wondered what else, exactly, was in there.

The good (and scary) thing about the Internet is that you can locate not just the answers to such questions, but also a lot of people who appear to have lived your same life. When I Googled "Yucca Flats," a great many cocktail blogs appeared containing such comments as "We drink this when we are playing cards" and "It's great for large groups . . . but it does sneak up on you." One post recommended mixing it with your feet. There was some disagreement about the recipe (versions included vodka, gin, rum, tequila, or some combination thereof), but the consensus seems to be that a Yucca Flats is a whole lot of gin mixed with equal parts lemon juice and sugar, shaken or stirred with ice until really, really cold, and augmented with maraschino cherries and several squeezed halves of lemons, limes, and oranges.

I'm not sure I'd mix it in a garbage can anymore, but I think the Yucca Flats could find renewed popularity in this cocktail-obsessed age in which seasonal drink lists are incorporated into bar lists across the country. Warm-weather months mean a change from brown liquor to white, from heavy cocktails to those that are lighter, fruitier, and more refreshing, though equally potent. The Flats certainly qualifies on that front, and it might also be considered part of the trend toward what master mixologist Dale DeGroff calls "a culinary style of cocktails, utilizing exotic fruit and kitchen ingredients." The kind of drinks DeGroff has in mind might include something like a lemon thyme margarita or a Rickshaw, the excellent drink at New York's Gramercy Tavern made from gin, lime juice, and basil syrup. But hey, my kitchen also has plenty of lemons, limes, and oranges, as well as maraschino cherries.

Below I include a recipe I found for a Yucca Flats that comes closest to the one of my memory. But my research also turned up the fact that people were enjoying a similar drink more than a century before my poker-playing days. Cocktail historian David Wondrich uncovered an 1862 edition of the world's first bartender's guide, *How to Mix Drinks, or The Bon-Vivant's Companion*, in which there's a recipe for Gin Punch that sounds a lot like the Yucca Flats, though it is for a single serving. Jason Kosmas and Dushan Zaric, the genius mix-masters behind Manhattan's Pravda, Members Only, and other game-changing bars, adapted the recipe to serve a crowd and added champagne to create what is essentially an upscale Yucca Flats. If you happen to be drinking alone, a gin sour is an elegant and delicious alternative.

No matter what its incarnation, the Flats will always remind me of those carefree, formative summers spent in the Yarbroughs' playroom. A few years ago, when Mrs. Yarbrough died, much of the old gang got together at her funeral and we vowed to have a memorial poker tournament in her honor. I already know what we will serve; the Allman Brothers will be on the playlist.

THE YUCCA FLATS

(*Yield: Depends on the crowd!*)

One 16-ounce box confectioners' sugar

2 fifths gin

One 6-ounce jar maraschino cherries, with juice

6 oranges, halved

6 limes, halved

6 lemons, halved

Dissolve sugar in the gin in a gallon-size glass jar. Add the remaining ingredients. Fill with ice. Wrap jar in a towel and take turns shaking until the mixture is really cold and some of the ice has melted.

GIN PUNCH

(*Yield: 5¾ quarts*)

Decorative ice ring (see page 133)

6 navel oranges, sliced and cut into quarter wheels

6 lemons, sliced and cut in half

3 limes, sliced

1 pint fresh raspberries

1 pineapple, cut into 1-inch cubes

1 bottle Plymouth Gin

1¾ cups freshly squeezed lemon juice

1¼ cups simple syrup

¼ cup orgeat syrup

1 cup Massenet crème de framboise

3 cups water

1 bottle Brut Champagne

Prepare decorative ice ring, allowing a few hours for freezing.

Combine all the fruits in a large punch bowl. Add gin, lemon juice, syrups, crème de framboise, and water. Refrigerate at least 4 to 5 hours. Just before serving, add the champagne and the decorative ice block.

GIN SOUR

(*Yield: 1 drink*)

1 ounce lemon juice

½ ounce simple syrup

2 ounces gin

Stemmed cherry, for garnish

Shake first three ingredients over ice cubes in a shaker. For a straight-up drink, strain into a cocktail glass. Otherwise, strain into a rocks glass and add ice. Either way, garnish with the cherry.

· 19 ·

Kentucky Sunshine

In the spring of 2012, the United States Court of Appeals for the Sixth Circuit issued a ruling in favor of Maker's Mark Distillery, protecting the red dripping wax seal the brand has used on its bottles since its introduction in 1958. Bill Samuels, Sr., whose family has produced bourbon whiskey in Kentucky pretty much continuously since the eighteenth century, formulated the recipe for Maker's Mark in 1953; his wife Margie came up with the idea of the seal and used the family deep fryer to perfect the method of applying it. Now owned by Jim Beam, Maker's Mark is still run by the Smith family (Bill Sr.'s grandson Rob is the current CEO), so in 2001 when Jose Cuervo started selling a premium tequila called Reserva de la Familia, with a seal almost identical to that of Maker's Mark, the brand struck back. The seal, referred to by the court as a "signature trade dress element," is, after all, a literal maker's mark. Also, no one wants to find out what would happen if a bottle of tequila were to be confused with one of bourbon.

I bring all this up because I have the high honor of being mentioned in the opinion, which was written by Judge Boyce F. Martin Jr., the most senior active judge on the court and my new hero. Martin makes the point that distillers began branding their bourbons early on, and he cites a *Newsweek* column I wrote mentioning that Ulysses S. Grant preferred Old Crow above all others. Thanks to Martin, I now know that Dr. James Crow, a Kentuckian by way of Scotland, is the man who perfected the sour mash method of whiskey making sometime between 1823 and 1845, and that he was one of the first makers to brand bourbon with his name.

Martin's ruling is a treasure trove of such information and required reading for anyone remotely interested in bourbon, the whiskey first produced in the late eighteenth century in the "Old Bourbon" region of Kentucky. Recognized by Congress in 1964 as "a distinct product of America," it must be made of a grain mixture that is at least 51 percent corn, distilled in America at less than 160 proof with nothing added but water, and aged for a minimum of two years in new, charred oak barrels. The corn is the thing. We'd all still be drinking Scotch or rye if it hadn't been for the fact that corn, a crop unknown to Europeans before Columbus turned up, was so easy to grow in Kentucky and somebody had to figure out what to do with the surplus.

To read the opinion is to imagine the fun Judge Martin's clerks must have had. Who knew that James Bond creator and martini aficionado Ian Fleming switched his allegiance to bourbon, or that Harry Truman started his day with a walk, a rubdown, a shot of bourbon, and a light breakfast?

Martin begins by quoting former Supreme Court Justice Hugo Black, an Alabama native, who wrote, "I was raised to believe that Scotch whisky would need a tax preference to survive in competition with Kentucky bourbon." It's a funny line—and useful to Martin, who turns it around in favor of Maker's Mark: "While there may be some truth to Justice Black's statement that Kentucky bourbon is such an economic force that its competitors need government protection or preference to compete with it, it does not mean a Kentucky bourbon distiller may not avail itself of our laws to protect its assets."

But Black's line struck me for another reason. I have never been so passionate about bourbon, and I have always felt slightly guilty about that fact. Bourbon is not just America's, but the South's greatest (and pretty much only) contribution to the world of spirits as well as a significant contribution to the wider cultural landscape. Not being in bourbon's camp is sort of like saying you don't like blues or jazz or Creole cooking, and it is a sin compounded by the fact that my spirit of choice has always been Scotch.

Walker Percy said drinking Scotch was like looking at a picture of Noël Coward; Faulkner said between Scotch and nothing, he'd take Scotch. When I first moved north, Yankees were forever handing me glasses of bourbon, figuring that if a Southerner wanted whiskey, it would surely be made from corn. As it happens, I know a lot of Southern Scotch drinkers, most of whom, in the Mississippi Delta at least, were weaned on John Handy, a brand with a Cutty Sark base that was then blended with New Orleans tap water by the same people who owned the local Schwegmann's grocery store chain. Mississippi was dry until 1966 and we were all at the mercy of what our bootlegger had on offer. In the case of Scotch, that was it.

Given the options, perhaps it's no wonder that many of our greatest citizens preferred bourbon. George Washington distilled bourbon at Mount Vernon, and Abraham Lincoln's father was a seasonal distillery hand. Henry Clay, John Calhoun, and Daniel Webster all drank bourbon, as did Mark Twain. Walker Percy wrote an oft-reprinted essay in praise of the stuff, but he was no connoisseur since his early life was spent in the same town in Mississippi that mine was and everybody had the same bootlegger. On the bourbon front, the stock was usually limited to Old Crow, the aforementioned favorite of Grant, as well as of our postman, for whom my mother left a bottle in the mailbox every Christmas.

Percy preferred Early Times—the protagonist in *Love in the Ruins* holes up in an abandoned Howard Johnson's with fifteen cases of it, along with three good-looking women and The World's Great Books—mainly, he said, because at 80 proof he could drink more of it. Percy would likely be amused at today's profusion of artisanal-style "small batch" bourbons, but in fact they recall bourbon's heyday at the opening of the twentieth century when almost two hundred brands, each with very distinct characteristics, vied for drinkers' approval.

Bourbon's individuality comes from the quality of the oak barrels in which it is aged and the environment in which they are stored, as well as the length of aging and final strength. The resulting range of nuances can be so varied that a tasting vocabulary not unlike the one ordinarily reserved for fine wine is used to describe them. Percy happily settled for "the little explosion of Kentucky U.S.A. sunshine in the cavity of the nasophayrnx," but were he alive to drink, say, a sixteen-year-old A. H. Hirsh Reserve, he might also detect, as one critic did, "smoky, floral aromas" and flavors of "fruit and chocolate." Likewise, Evan Williams Single Barrel Vintage 1998 is said to boast aromas of "brown banana, cloves, and glove leather," while twelve-year-old W. L. Weller has a "complex and toasty palate" and a "sweet and oaky" finish.

My favorite, twenty-year-old Pappy van Winkle's Family Reserve, is as suave and rich as a fine brandy, and mind-blowing enough to have brought me around to the bourbon camp. I'm almost as happy with the comparatively inexpensive Knob Creek or Basil Hayden's, sipped neat from a heavy glass. I think the reason I abhorred bourbon in the first place was that for years everybody I knew drank it with Coke.

These days, the national cocktail craze that has coincided with the explosion of small batch bourbons has sent folks back into the archives for more interesting and complex bourbon cocktails, including the whiskey smashes below. The smash is a drink that hails from what historian David Wondrich refers to as the cocktail's "Baroque Age," which ranged from 1830 to 1885, about the same time that Dr. Crow was perfecting bourbon. I was served my first whiskey smash at Commander's Palace a few years ago by Lally Brennan and Ti Martin, the remarkable cousins who run the New Orleans landmark. Before it occurred to me that the whiskey in question would not be Scotch, I took a sip and both my mind and palate were immediately opened. In response, I've attempted to open the palate of many a lifelong bourbon drinker with my version of a Scotch old fashioned, but holdouts needn't worry—the recipe is just fine with bourbon. Finally, I can find few holdouts against the fig-infused bourbon toddy from my friends Chris and Idie Hastings at Birmingham's Hot and Hot Fish Club. Lately people have been infusing bourbon with everything from bacon to apples and cinnamon, but this infusion is a fine regional pairing that also makes a good drink.

Now a convert, I realize that bourbon, with or without the fig, is a wholly American and appropriate indulgence. Dr. Tom More, the Percy character who took refuge with Early Times, was doing so because in the "dread latter days of the old violent beloved U.S.A.," pure "wickedness" abounded in "high places" and all hell had broken loose; he was anticipating nothing less than the end of the world. If that scenario sounds scarily familiar, take heart. At the novel's end, not only is the world still intact, More has married the best of the three women and is outside on his patio, merrily barbecuing a turkey on Christmas Eve. His accompaniments are the songs of Sinatra and several restorative shots of bourbon. There are worse remedies, as I'm sure the esteemed Judge Martin would agree, though it is unclear from his opinion whether he drinks the stuff. I looked him up and he was born in Boston, but he went to Davidson College and the University of Virginia law school and he's lived in Louisville for all his adult life, so I suspect so. He's also taken courageous stances against the death penalty in a pro-penalty state, so I also suspect he could use a shot or two at the end of the day. Next time I pour my own, I intend to raise a glass to him.

THE COMMANDER'S PALACE WHISKEY SMASH

(*Yield: 1 drink*)

3 lemon wedges

4 fresh spearmint leaves

1 ounce orange curaçao

2 ounces bourbon

1 sprig fresh spearmint, for garnish

Muddle the lemon wedges, spearmint leaves, and curaçao in a bar glass or shaker. Add the bourbon and ice and shake well. Strain the drink into a rocks glass filled with ice and garnish with the mint sprig.

WHISKEY SMASH 2

(*Yield: 1 drink*)

2 orange wheels

3 or 4 fresh mint leaves

½ ounce mint simple syrup

2 to 3 ounces of the best bourbon you can find

1 sprig mint, for garnish

Fill a rocks glass with shaved or crushed ice and tuck orange slices inside so that they cover the sides of the glass. In the bottom of a shaker, stir mint leaves with mint syrup, tapping on the leaves to release their essence. Add bourbon and ice cubes and shake vigorously. Pour into the prepared glass and garnish with mint sprig.

NOTE: This cocktail is a wonderful and slightly more complex alternative to a mint julep. To make the mint syrup, simply boil 1 cup sugar and 1 cup water for a few minutes until sugar has dissolved. Remove from heat and throw in 1 bunch of mint. Let steep for about 30 minutes, strain through a fine mesh sieve, and refrigerate.

MY OLD FASHIONED

(*Yield: 1 drink*)

1 large Meyer lemon or orange peel, scraped to remove as much pith as possible

1 sugar cube (preferably La Perruche brand)

3 to 4 dashes Fee Brothers Orange Bitters

3 to 4 dashes Fee Brothers Old Fashioned Bitters

3 ounces Scotch

1 orange slice, for garnish

In a rocks glass, muddle peel, sugar cube with the bitters, and about 2 teaspoons of cold water. Swirl to make sure liquid coats glass. Add ice and whiskey, stir well, and garnish with orange slice.

THE HOT AND HOT FISH CLUB'S
FIG-INFUSED SMALL BATCH BOURBON
(*Yield: 1 750ml bottle*)

1 pound fresh ripe figs, such as brown turkey, mission, or
    celeste
1 (750ml) bottle good quality small batch bourbon, such as
    Basil Hayden

Wash the figs well under warm running water and pat dry. Remove the stems and cut into quarters. Place the quartered figs into a 3-quart sterilized jar. Add the bourbon to the jar, reserving the original bourbon bottle, and secure the top of the jar. Allow the bourbon to sit in a cool, dry place for at least 2 weeks or until the bourbon has a distinct fig aroma and flavor.

Strain the infusion through a fine-meshed sieve into a clean container. Place the bourbon-soaked figs into an airtight container in the refrigerator and reserve for the Fig-Infused Bourbon "Toddy." Pour the infused bourbon back into the reserved bourbon bottle. The bourbon is ready to use and will keep, at room temperature, for up to 1 year.

FIG-INFUSED BOURBON "TODDY"
(*Yield: 1 drink*)

1½ ounces fig-infused bourbon

½ bourbon-soaked fig, cut into quarters

1 cup ice

1 preserved fig or maraschino cherry, for garnish

Combine the bourbon, bourbon-soaked fig, and the ice in a
martini shaker and muddle until the fig is well mashed and the
ice is somewhat crushed. Pour the mixture into a rocks glass
and garnish with the preserved fig or cherry.

· 20 ·

The Morning After

There comes a time in every drinker's life when he or she is in need of a reviver, a pick-me-up, something to restore interest in living to see another day, maybe even eating a little something. Fortunately, much research has been devoted to the subject. In Charles H. Baker, Jr.'s *Exotic Drink Book* (volume two of *The Gentleman's Companion*), he offers up no less than "twenty and seven picker uppers," a "hand-culled little list of variegated hairs of the dog" ranging from a Swiss Yodeler (a jigger of absinthe shaken with an egg white and a teaspoon of anisette) to a Peking Tiger's Milk No. 1 (essentially a milk punch made with the best cognac you can afford).

Baker, whose volume is subtitled *Around the World with Jigger, Beaker and Flask,* writes that his carefully chosen picker-uppers "not only enable us to greet the new day undismayed but may—on occasion—save a life." The same miracle-working qualities are ascribed to the "patent morning revivers" created by Jeeves, the ever-resourceful "gentleman's personal gentleman," employed by London's bumbling man-about-town

Bertie Wooster. In *Jeeves Takes Charge,* one of P. G. Wode-
house's earliest stories featuring the two characters, Bertie is
afflicted with an especially painful "morning head" and hires
Jeeves after he's been cured by the valet's "tissue-restorer," an
extra fiery version of a prairie oyster. Its immediate effects are
a tad rough: "For a moment, I felt as if somebody had touched
off a bomb inside the old bean and was strolling down my
throat with a lighted torch." In subsequent rematches, Bertie's
skull flies toward the ceiling and his eyes "rebound from the
opposite wall like racquet balls," but the onslaught is invariably pronounced worth it. "The sun shone in through the
window; birds twittered in the treetops; and, generally speak-
ing, hope dawned once more."

Still, getting there remains a touchy business. W. C. Fields
once refused a proffered Bromo Seltzer by explaining that he
couldn't stand the noise. When Kingsley Amis decided to treat
a "kingly hangover" with bicarbonate of soda and a vodka
chaser, his companion put the same combo in a glass as a dem-
onstration of what was likely going on in Amis's stomach: "The
mixture turned black and gave off smoke." Better, then, to
ease into things without wreaking quite so much violence.

Having learned his lesson, Amis suggests sex, water, a series
of hot baths and showers, followed by a "tuft" of the dog that
bit you. Among Baker's favored "tufts" is "the refreshing chill
tartness" of a very large, very cold champagne cocktail (preferably the Imperial Cossack Crusta), an admitted expense justi-
fied by the alternative: "a 'turn' from the sight of a raw egg or
the taste of sweet ingredients." Evelyn Waugh discovered his
own champagne remedy, "an almost unendurably desirable
drink," after a late night in Athens with some "charming Nor-
wegians." A large sugar cube is soaked in Angostura bitters,

rolled in cayenne pepper, and placed in a roomy glass, which is then filled with champagne. "Each bubble as it rises to the surface carries with it a red grain of pepper," Waugh wrote, "so that as one drinks, one's appetite is at once stimulated and gratified, heat and cold, fire and liquid, contending on one's palate and alternating in the mastery of one's sensations."

I am all for similar stimulation and gratification, but I needn't be inspired to the same level of poetic rapture of the gentlemen above. What I'm looking for is a drink that not only tames the ills of the previous evening but induces a certain amount of stamina, along with equal measures of charm and affability—the kind needed to get through such alcohol-laden occasions as Mardi Gras, festive house parties or road trips, and long wedding weekends. To this end I frequently employ the comparatively prosaic Bloody Mary, but only if it's the one made from fresh-squeezed tomato juice at Sylvain in New Orleans's French Quarter or the recipe perfected by my mother, who uses almost as much lime as tomato juice. A rocky morning is no time for a concoction as thick and over-seasoned as a bottle of Ragú, nor does one need a salad—lemon wedge, olive, bean, pickled pepper, whatever—all but blocking the intake of the Bloody. A lovely pale yellow stalk of celery from the tender heart of the bunch is an appropriate garnish, as is a single spear of pickled okra. Otherwise let it go.

Another of my favorite restoratives is the Bullshot, a perfect combination of beef bouillon and vodka created at Bangkok's Rama Hotel and introduced to me by the late gardener/socialite C. Z. Guest, who added a genius stroke in the form of freshly grated horseradish. The horseradish provides a less abusive bite than the concoctions of Jeeves and Amis, and the beef stock provides a nourishing dose of protein that is also kind to the tummy. The key is stock that is very rich but very clear, and Polish or Russian vodka that is very good and very cold.

A healthy amount of chilled vodka also is important to the latest—and possibly the greatest—reviver that I've found. Called a St. Cloud, it was discovered in the lovely Boston bistro Aquitaine by my friends Carl and Amanda Cottingham, with whom I grew up in Mississippi. Carl and Amanda were smart enough to line up dozens of Pimm's Cups on silver trays as readily accessible revivers during a brunch they threw during my own very long wedding weekend. I trust them on all matters of food and drink, so that when Carl told me what was in the St. Cloud—vodka, fresh grapefruit juice, and rosemary simple syrup—I mixed one up at once. The cocktail has since saved my own life and those of countless others and is now the house (morning) drink. Such are its powers that I went to Boston (ostensibly on other business) to taste it, a mission that turned me on to the origin of the name (the restaurant was originally called the St. Cloud) as well as a fourth ingredient (lime zest grated over the top).

Since rosemary is said to quicken the metabolism, strengthen the stomach, and act as a decongestant, the St. Cloud has clear medicinal qualities. There's also all that vitamin C in the grapefruit juice. Beyond that, it is utterly delicious and, imbibed judiciously, definitely increases the charm factor.

ST. CLOUD

(*Yield: 1 drink*)

2 cups water

2 cups sugar

A handful of rosemary branches

5 or 6 ounces freshly squeezed grapefruit juice, strained and chilled

2 ounces vodka, well chilled

Freshly grated lime zest

Make a simple syrup by boiling 2 cups sugar and 2 cups water for a few minutes until the sugar is completely dissolved. Take the pot off the heat and steep a healthy handful of rosemary branches in the syrup. Leave it on the counter to cool with the herbs for 30 minutes to an hour. Remove branches and strain syrup. This will keep refrigerated in a jar for at least a month, which is why I always make at least 2 cups of the stuff.

While the syrup is cooling, squeeze fresh grapefruits (the Ruby Red variety is sweetest and prettiest) to make as much juice as you need. Strain through a wire mesh strainer, and chill.

For one drink, put 2 ounces of vodka in a highball glass and top with grapefruit juice. Stir in a couple of tablespoons of the rosemary syrup and taste (depending on the sweetness of the juice, you may need more). Grate lime zest over the top and garnish with a rosemary sprig.

NOTE: If you want to get fancy, shake the 2 ounces of vodka with 5 ounces of grapefruit juice and 2 tablespoons of simple syrup in a shaker filled with ice. Strain into a chilled stemmed glass and taste to see if it needs more syrup before grating the lime zest over the top. I also do the math and make these in quantities large enough for pitchers to serve at brunches and other gatherings.

IMPERIAL COSSACK CRUSTA

(*Yield: 1 drink*)

1 lime

Powdered sugar

2 dashes orange bitters (preferably Fee Brothers)

2 ounces cognac

1 ounce kummel, chilled

Champagne, chilled

Cut the lime in half lengthwise and rub both sides of each half (to release both the oils and the juices) on the entire inside of a large stemmed cocktail or wineglass, as well as around the rim and about a half-inch down below the rim on the outside. Dip the lip in powdered sugar, then fill the whole glass with sugar. Empty out the sugar and allow what sticks to remain.

To a bar glass with three ice cubes, add the bitters, cognac, and kummel, and stir. Pour the mixture into the prepared glass and top with chilled champagne.

NOTE: Kummel is a delicious clear liqueur flavored with caraway seed, fennel, and cumin.

BULLSHOT

(*Yield: 1 drink*)

4 ounces beef bouillon

1 teaspoon lemon juice

1 or 2 dashes Worcestershire sauce

1 to 2 dashes Tabasco sauce

2 ounces vodka

Freshly grated horseradish

Pour the bouillon, lemon juice, Worcestershire, and Tabasco into a cocktail shaker filled with ice. Add vodka and shake. Strain into a highball glass and grate horseradish over the top. Stir gently and serve.

NOTE: No one wants a Bullshot with even a trace of fat in the bouillon—chilled fat is a most unpleasant sensation. The trick is to make a good homemade stock (flavored with onion, celery, and parsley—no carrots) and degrease it thoroughly. (Chill, remove the layer of hard fat on the surface, and strain twice through 3 layers of cheesecloth.)

JUDY'S BLOODY MARY MIX

(*Yield: Enough for about 8 cocktails*)

One 46-ounce can tomato juice

1¼ cups freshly squeezed lime juice

½ cup Worcestershire sauce

4 healthy dashes Tabasco

1 tablespoon salt

Freshly ground black pepper

1 tablespoon prepared horseradish

Put first five ingredients in a pitcher and stir well. Add pepper to taste and stir in horseradish.

CORPSE REVIVER NO. 2

(*Yield: 1 cocktail*)

1 ounce gin

1 ounce Cointreau

1 ounce Lillet blanc

1 ounce lemon juice

⅛ teaspoon Pernod or absinthe

1 maraschino cherry, stem removed, for garnish

Fill a stemmed glass with ice to chill. In a cocktail shaker, combine the first five ingredients and shake vigorously. Empty ice from the martini glass and pour in strained mixture from shaker. Garnish with cherry.

NOTE: There are many versions of the Corpse Reviver No. 2, but this one from *The Savoy Cocktail Book of 1930* by Harry Craddock is a classic. Don't forget to heed Craddock's warning: "Four of these taken in swift succession will unrevive the corpse again."

...AND MAKING MERRY

· 21 ·

A Happy Enchilada

Last night, thunderstorms, high winds, and hail ravaged areas in and around New Orleans. This morning, my windows are wide open and I'm looking out at one of the most beautiful days I've ever seen. It's the kind of day that allows people to forget the impending hurricane season and summer's steamy slog. There's absolutely no humidity and the sky is a cloudless deep blue. The sweet olives have just popped and the scent is everywhere; the dog is in his usual spot on the second-floor balcony. I've already—almost—forgotten the fact that the latest guaranteed repair on my permanently leaking sunroom flat roof typically did not hold, or that last week after a similar storm, St. Charles Avenue was briefly a river. I once wrote that living in New Orleans was like living in the Old Testament, but right this minute I'm not thinking about the pestilence and plagues and manmade mayhem that are sure to be around the corner.

Such are the vicissitudes of life down here—and pretty much everywhere else. It's like the lyrics of the John Prine song: "You're up one day, the next you're down; It's a half an inch of water and you think you're gonna drown; That's the way that the world goes round." There are a lot of things I love about that song, not least of which is a story Prine tells about a woman who once requested it at a concert. She'd misheard the words "half an inch of water" and asked him to play "that happy enchilada song." How great a metaphor is that? Who in the world wouldn't want a happy enchilada, bursting with all kinds of good stuff?

Today, then, is a happy enchilada day. We are not, for a change, drowning, but waving. That last line, of course, is a play on the Stevie Smith poem *Not Waving but Drowning,* and it is not, I admit, original. When my friend, the writer and editor Henry Allen, gave me a volume of Smith's poems several years ago, he inscribed it, "To Julia, Who is not drowning, but waving." It was among the best compliments I've ever received and by far the best book inscription. It's also a good philosophy to cling to on most days no matter where you live, but especially here, where a half an inch of water would be the good news.

The first time I heard John Prine live was at the Greenville (Mississippi) High School auditorium when I was thirteen and he was barely famous. Kenneth Haxton, the director of our local symphony who delighted in stirring up trouble, slipped him into the fall lineup between an opera singer and a piano soloist. The unsuspecting season ticket holders, including a lot of old ladies in chiffon and mink, valiantly stuck it out. The few Baptists in attendance exited en masse when Prine got to the line in "Sam Stone" about Jesus Christ dying "for nothing, I suppose," but then irony and context have never been their strong suits. The rest of us could not believe our luck.

I saw Prine again more than thirty years later at Jazz Fest in New Orleans, (where he performed, rather fittingly, in the rain), but during the years in between I heard his music played more times than I can count in the living room of the house where I grew up. My family's been mightily blessed to have a great many close friends of all generations who are far more musically talented than we are, and to this day, we seldom have a party that doesn't morph into an impromptu concert. My friend Ralph McGee has always been a huge Prine fan—he and his wife Ann were in the front row of the auditorium for that concert in Greenville, and he played "Illegal Smile" for me when I was too young to figure out what it meant. Ralph is also a seriously gifted guitar player, and he and his brother Humphreys both have great voices. At almost every gathering they crack everybody up with Prine's "Four Way Stop Dilemma," always my father's number one request, and they never fail to break my heart with "Hello In There."

Humphreys and Ralph's father, Ug, played the guitar at a dinner party my parents had for Bill Buckley and his wife Pat when they visited Greenville, a raucous evening that ended with Buckley pounding out *"Cielito Lindo"* on the piano while Ug's daughter Chargee danced on the table. I was eleven then, but we have not stopped showing off for outsiders. When I threw a party for then British ambassador to the United States Sir Christopher Meyer and his wife Catherine several years ago, the McGee brothers rose to the occasion with a rousing performance of "Happy Enchilada" (otherwise known as "That's the Way the World Goes 'Round"). Sir Christopher was making an official visit to Mississippi and my assignment was to provide a festive diversion before the dull stuff. We had a catfish fry at a juke in Panther Burn where Ralph farms; we ate steaks and hot tamales at Doe's Eat Place. The night of the party, Ralph and Ann's son and daughter-in-law, both just off stints as chefs in two of New Orleans's best restaurants, dazzled everyone with a regional feast that included lots of crabmeat and barbecued oysters and the Brits went back home well fed and well entertained.

When I'm in the kitchen without the benefit of professional chefs, we usually have a one-pot meal and a big salad so everyone can eat on their laps, often on the floor around the fireplace in front of which the musicians always pull up a stool or two. One of my more popular standbys is crawfish étouffée. As it happens, there's a restaurant in Breaux Bridge, Louisiana, the wonderful Café des Amis, which serves crawfish enchiladas—essentially tortillas filled with étouffée and topped with cheese. I serve my own étouffée with rice and lots of French bread and a big salad with a make-ahead dressing that is one of my long-time favorites. Dessert is "pick-up," too—usually my mother's famous lemon squares. She gilds the lily by icing the baked lemon filling rather than sprinkling it with powdered sugar, and people have been known to stuff them in their pockets. No matter what we actually eat, those evenings are nothing short of soul-feeding—very happy enchiladas indeed.

CRAWFISH ÉTOUFFÉE

(*Yield: 8 servings*)

SEASONING MIX

2 teaspoons salt

2 teaspoons cayenne pepper

1 teaspoon white pepper

1 teaspoon black pepper

1 teaspoon dried basil

2 teaspoons dried thyme

¼ cup chopped onion

¼ cup chopped celery

¼ cup chopped green bell pepper

7 tablespoons Wesson oil

¾ cup all-purpose flour

3 cups seafood stock

2 tablespoons tomato paste

1 cup (2 sticks) butter

2 pounds peeled crawfish tails or medium shrimp

1 cup finely chopped green onions

¼ cup cognac

3 or 4 healthy dashes of Worcestershire sauce

In one small bowl, thoroughly blend seasoning mix ingredients. In another bowl, combine chopped onion, celery, and bell pepper.

In a large heavy-bottomed saucepan or Dutch oven, heat the oil over high heat until it begins to smoke, about 4 minutes. Using a metal whisk, gradually whisk in flour, beating constantly to keep from scorching. Make sure to eliminate any lumps and keep beating for 3 to 5 minutes, or until the roux turns a sort of medium reddish brown. Remove from heat and immediately dump in the chopped vegetables. Stir in 1 tablespoon of the seasoning mix and keep stirring, off heat, until vegetables have softened and cooked a bit, about 4 minutes.

Slowly whisk in the stock while bringing to a boil, making sure the roux is fully dissolved. Lower to a simmer, add the tomato paste, and continue to simmer for about 25 minutes. By this time the paste will be well incorporated and the flour taste all gone. Remove from heat.

In a large skillet or saucepan, heat 1 stick of the butter. Add crawfish (or shrimp) and green onions and sauté for about 2 or 3 minutes, stirring constantly. Turn the fire under the stock/roux mixture to medium and stir in the crawfish mixture. Add the cognac and remaining stick of butter. Stir until butter melts. Stir in one more tablespoon of the seasoning mix and taste. Add more, depending on the heat level you prefer. Serve immediately, or keep warm over very low heat, stirring occasionally so that it doesn't separate.

NOTE: I have made this recipe for as many as eighty people—or ten times the original recipe—with no problem. I learned the hard way that you do not need to multiply the pepper, or even the salt, by the same amount, only the dried herbs. Make up the seasoning mix as for one batch, and add extra herbs and a little extra salt. After you add the crawfish toward the end, you can figure out how much more heat the dish needs. The trick is to taste and taste again—you may need a touch more tomato paste or cognac, or thyme or Worcestershire. Just taste— that's the key to all "stew-y" dishes like this.

FRENCH DRESSING

(*Yield: About 2½ cups*)

1½ cups Wesson oil (you may also use safflower or canola)

½ cup red wine vinegar

½ cup sugar

2 teaspoons curry powder

½ onion, sliced

Juice of 1 lemon

½ teaspoon salt

Pinch of cayenne pepper

½ teaspoon Worcestershire sauce

Mix all ingredients together and let stand for 24 hours. Remove onion before using.

NOTE: I copied this recipe, simply titled "French Dressing," from my mother's own notebook when I left home for college. Everybody loves it and no one can ever figure out that what they're tasting in it is curry. It's wonderful on a composed salad of Boston lettuce, red onion, grapefruit, and avocado, which has long been a holiday staple in our house. For big parties like the one described above, I toss a mix of Boston, romaine, watercress, and, occasionally, iceberg with sliced red onion, avocado, and sliced hearts of palm.

JUDY'S ICED LEMON SQUARES
(*Yield: About 16 squares*)

FOR THE CRUST

2 cups flour

½ cup powdered sugar

1½ sticks butter, at room temperature

FOR THE FILLING

2 cups sugar

4 eggs

1 tablespoon flour

½ teaspoon baking powder

6 tablespoons lemon juice

Grated rind of one lemon

FOR THE ICING

2 tablespoons melted butter

1 cup powdered sugar

1 tablespoon lemon juice

Preheat the oven to 350 degrees.

Sift flour and sugar together and cut in butter until well blended. Press into ungreased 8 × 12-inch baking pan. Bake for 15 minutes until lightly browned. Leave oven on.

Whisk together filling ingredients. Pour over baked crust and bake for 25 minutes. Cool.

Melt butter and stir in powdered sugar and lemon juice until smooth. Spread a thin coat over the baked and cooled filling. Let set and cut into squares.

· 22 ·

Table Talk

During the many years that I lived in New York, I grew to fear two words above all others: Table Talk. You might be seated at a perfectly nice dinner table, trying valiantly to make conversation with your neighbor (and occasionally succeeding) when the host or hostess taps on his or her glass and announces that it is time to turn our attention to the pressing issues of the day. Sometimes, the phrase "table talk" is actually used, sometimes not. Either way, small talk, flirting, witty asides, pretty much everything that makes a dinner party bearable or even fun, comes to an abrupt halt and a topic is introduced—a recent Supreme Court ruling, say, or the fate of the latest immigration bill. The guests are then made to take turns around the table saying what they think about it.

In me, this brings up fear and loathing and torturous memories of my six weeks at a Christian camp in Alabama where the counselors went around the cabin after lights out and made us all tell God—out loud—what we were thankful for. In everyone else, apparently, it brings out new levels of pomposity and long-windedness and all sorts of other things best left out of dinner parties.

During one especially excruciating session at the apartment of a TV executive and former cabinet secretary, the topic was the Gaza Strip. When it was his turn to say his bit (and I emphasize the word "bit"), one of the guests who had recently returned from the region just kept on talking. (This same man had been my dinner partner at a previous party where he regaled me with jokes he read off cards taken out of his wallet, so I had already braced myself.) Anyway, I have a lot of thoughts on the Gaza Strip myself, all wildly different from this guy's, but even if I had wanted to respond to him, I couldn't have. This is the thing about table talk—it completely shuts down spontaneity and lively debate and, worse, the flow of wine. In this particular case, not even the waiter was allowed to cross into the lofty oratory zone.

Impeded by nothing, the speaker droned on and on, until I got busy devising ways to somehow vanish beneath the table. Finally, there was a timid knock on the dining room door—a still-very-much-with-it-and-adorable Brooke Astor also was in attendance and her minder had standing orders to come and fetch her at ten P.M. no matter what. This did not stop the droning, alas. But it did make me wish more than anything in the world that I had a minder—and I have never been more jealous of anyone in my life than the happily departing Mrs. Astor.

Writing this reminds me of a dinner party a few years ago at my mother's house in Seaside, Florida. At the time, the Ogden Museum of Southern Art in New Orleans, where I sit on the board, had a "satellite" in the next-door community called Watercolor, and my great friend William Dunlap, the artist and the most unreconstructed liberal I know, had just had an opening. His old college buddy, who is far, far to the right of him (and, indeed, to pretty much everyone), came to the house afterward, along with some devoted arts supporters, a restaurateur/columnist/cookbook author, an architect, and assorted other friends, including Joyce Wilson, who had spearheaded the Ogden at Watercolor. After we sat down, the right-winger made one of the arts supporters so mad that at one point she rose from her chair and looked like she might be about to hit him. Several of us pelted Dunlap with napkins after he said Al Gore was a terrible candidate but would have made a great president.

We drank a lot of wine—which never quit flowing—and ate grilled Roman steaks and a dish I made up with warm field peas and enormous Gulf shrimp in a sherry wine vinaigrette. I can't remember what we had for dessert, but afterward we took the wine out on the porch and someone let the dog out, which made me so briefly hysterical I began pelting poor Dunlap again when he told me everything would be all right. It was—we found the pup at my neighbors' house feasting on hamburger buns, so we toasted his safe return and kept talking and laughing and listening to too-loud music until late into the night.

It turned out to be such a memorable occasion that the restaurateur/columnist wrote about it. To me it was not all that notable, just the norm—or at least what should be the norm. People should get in good old-fashioned arguments rather than raptly—sycophantically—listen to each other orate. They should fuss at each other, charm each other, and flirt, a lot, for God's sake, all in good fun, and make their partners laugh without the benefit of wallet-sized prompters.

I am firmly against the choreography of conversation—or the "anchoring" of parties, as one long-suffering friend puts it—by someone who makes like (or indeed happens to be) an anchorman.

I know very few people who aren't under a lot of stress right now. And I can think of no better remedy than to commune at the end of the day with good food and drink, to kick up your heels (or at least take them off under the table) with people you already love or might really want to get to know. With that in mind, Joyce and I threw another dinner party in Seaside not long ago. She had some friends she wanted me to meet, and our friend Karen Wagner, whose Meyer lemon trees are legendary, had infused an enormous jar of vodka with countless slices of the lemons, and she said she'd bring it over. The Seaside farmers' market had lots of lady peas and pink eye peas on offer that morning, so I repeated the field pea and shrimp salad, which is essentially a Southern riff on the white bean and shrimp antipasto always on offer at Nino, the restaurant in Rome that is one of my favorites in the world. Nino also is known for its Roman steaks, so I made those again too, along with some crabmeat bruschetta to start off. Joyce brought a seriously delicious flourless chocolate cake and I'd made some simple syrup with lavender sugar and infused it with mint, so we added it to the whipped cream that we served with the cake—which, I have to say, was inspired.

Karen's vodka was an enormous hit. Her husband Steve mixed it with ginger beer for a lemony Moscow Mule, and I mixed it with the lavender mint syrup and topped it with club soda. Both were delicious, as was the lemonade I made with the same syrup, to which, of course, we added more of the vodka. This time the dog stayed safely inside, but we found plenty of other things to toast—and talk about—without any pesky direction.

CRABMEAT BRUSCHETTA

(*Yield: 8 servings*)

8 generous slices crusty bread, preferable from a round country loaf or a fat loaf of sour dough, sliced about ¾ inch thick (if a wide loaf can't be found, use a baguette and double the amount of slices)

2 garlic cloves, halved

1 pound lump crabmeat (this is one of the few times that jumbo lump is not preferred; even backfin would be just fine)

⅓ cup good olive oil, plus more for the toast

Juice and zest of 1 lemon

1 jalapeño, seeded and chopped fine

Coarse salt

Prepare a fire on the grill or preheat the broiler.

Grill or broil the bread slices for about 30 seconds on each side, until crisp and golden brown (you want some grill marks or brown bits to appear, but be careful not to burn it). Rub one side of the bread with the cut side of the garlic and drizzle or brush with a little olive oil. If you are using the big slices from a round loaf, cut them in half.

Drain and pick over the crab and place in a mixing bowl. Add the olive oil and lemon juice and zest and toss carefully. Add the jalapeño and salt to taste. Spoon on top of the toast and serve.

WARM FIELD PEA AND SHRIMP SALAD

(*Yield: 8 to 10 servings*)

FOR THE PEAS

2 pounds peas (I like pink-eyes, crowders, and lady peas best for this, and you can combine them if desired)

2 onions, halved

3 bay leaves

4 thyme sprigs

1 rosemary sprig

3 dried hot chile peppers

2 teaspoons salt

Chicken stock or water

FOR THE SHRIMP

2 pounds large shrimp, peeled (and deveined if you are so inclined)

3 cups of water

2 tablespoons kosher salt

Freshly ground white pepper

1 tablespoon olive oil

FOR THE SALAD

2 or 3 shallots, diced finely

1 bunch arugula

Sherry vinegar, about 2 tablespoons

Olive oil, about 6 tablespoons (the best you can find is
    important in this recipe)

Salt

Freshly ground black pepper

1 bunch basil, cut into a chiffonade

Put peas and seasonings in a large pot and add stock or water
until peas are covered by 2 or 3 inches. Bring to a boil, reduce
heat to low, and simmer, uncovered, until peas are tender,
usually about 30 to 45 minutes. (You might need to skim some
foam off the top as they cook.) Cooking time will depend on the
type of pea and the age, so keep checking.

While peas are cooking, place shrimp shells in a pan, cover
them with about 3 cups water, and bring to a boil. Decrease the
heat to a simmer and cook about 20 minutes. Remove and
discard shells and taste stock for intensity. Return stock to a
healthy simmer and reduce until you have about a cup of
fragrant stock (see note on the following page).

Meanwhile, place the shelled shrimp in a bowl and rub and
toss 1 tablespoon of the salt. Wash under cold running water,
roughly pat dry, and rub and toss again with the remaining
tablespoon of salt. Rinse again, drain in a colander, and pat
dry. Sprinkle with the white pepper and toss.

When peas are done, remove from heat and strain. Immediately add the shallots and arugula and toss with about 2 tablespoons of sherry vinegar (the arugula will wilt a bit, which is what you want). Add about 6 tablespoons of olive oil along with salt and pepper and taste to make sure the oil/vinegar balance is right.

In a large sauté pan, heat 1 tablespoon of olive oil over medium-high heat until it begins to shimmer. Add the shrimp and cook until pink and opaque, about 3 to 5 minutes. Be careful not to overcook—as soon as one turns pink, taste it.

Toss the shrimp and basil leaves in the salad.

NOTE: I used to add shelled boiled shrimp to the peas, but once I discovered my friend Virginia Willis's method for cooking shrimp for a similar salad of corn in her excellent book, *Basic to Brilliant Y'all*, I do it her way. Salting and sautéing the shrimp adds an extra layer of flavor that is worth the tiny bit of extra work. You also have the bonus of the reduced shrimp stock. You can add a bit straight into the salad or really gild the lily by mixing a bit of it into homemade mayonnaise (see recipe on page 85) and serving a dollop on the side. The trick with this salad—as with so many things—is to "toss and taste." You might want more or less shallots; you might need more oil or vinegar. Sometimes I add chopped parsley if I have it. It's up to you.

ROMAN STEAKS

(*Yield: 4 to 6 servings*)

2 ribeye steaks, cut about 1½ to 2 inches thick

Coarse salt

Freshly ground black pepper

1 tablespoon finely chopped fresh rosemary

2 garlic cloves, peeled and chopped

½ cup good olive oil

1 lemon

Prepare a fire on the grill.

Season steaks generously with salt and pepper. In a small bowl, mix the rosemary and garlic with the oil, mashing with a spoon to make a rough paste. Spread on steaks and refrigerate for at least a couple of hours. (I try to do it on the morning before I cook that evening or, even better, overnight.)

Remove meat from the refrigerator in time for it to reach room temperature. Grill over hot coals until desired doneness, place on a cutting board, and squeeze the lemon over them. Cut into thick slices and place on warmed serving dish.

JOYCE'S FLAWLESS FLOURLESS CHOCOLATE CAKE

(*Yield: 6 to 8 servings*)

4 ounces fine-quality 70 percent chocolate

8 tablespoons (1 stick) butter

¾ cup sugar

3 large eggs, lightly beaten

½ cup unsweetened cocoa powder

Preheat the oven to 375 degrees and butter an 8-inch round baking pan. Line bottom with a round of wax paper and butter the paper.

Chop chocolate into small pieces. In a double boiler or metal bowl set over a saucepan of barely simmering water, melt the chocolate with butter, stirring until smooth. Remove top of double boiler or bowl from heat and whisk the sugar into the chocolate mixture. Add eggs and whisk well. Sift cocoa powder over chocolate mixture and whisk until just combined.

Pour batter into pan and bake in middle of oven for 25 minutes, or until top has formed a thin crust. Cool cake in the pan on a rack for 5 minutes and invert onto a serving plate.

NOTE: After being cooled completely, the cake will keep in an airtight container for one week.

LAVENDER MINT SYRUP

(*Yield: 2 cups*)

1 cup water
1 cup lavender sugar
1 bunch mint

Combine water and sugar in a saucepan and boil just until the sugar has dissolved. Remove pan from heat and submerge the mint in the syrup.

Let sit at least 30 minutes. Strain the syrup twice. When it has cooled, store in the refrigerator.

NOTE: Lavender sugar can be found in gourmet stores, including the wonderful Cardullo's in Cambridge, Massachusetts. The brand I use, Little Sky, is available on their Web site, www.cardullos.com.

· 23 ·

Shellfish Chic

The summer after my sophomore year in college,
I gave a dinner for a visiting Georgetown classmate on the terrace in front of the pool house in my parents' big backyard. I'm pretty sure it was August, so I can't imagine why we ate outside, except maybe because my parents were inside, and I was pretending I had a life—and a house—of my own. Anyway, my friend's name was Alexis and I didn't know her well, but she was at such loose ends after a breakup with her boyfriend that I asked her to come home with me for a week. Then I wondered what in the world I was going to do with her.

She spoke fluent French and German, she already had a job offer at a Swiss bank (in Switzerland!), and she'd grown up in Los Angeles, where she'd gone to high school with the children of Hollywood royalty. It turned out that the comparatively exotic terrain of the Mississippi Delta was plenty to keep her entertained, but just to make sure, I made a guest list of the coolest people I could round up and a menu that was suited to the heat but also suitably elegant. Looking back, it cracks me up that I was trying so hard for this girl, but, really, we do this stuff mostly for ourselves. And since I was already an inveterate clipper of magazines, I had a sheaf of recipes from the old *House & Garden* food section that I was dying to try.

The dinner began with a cold cream of cucumber and avocado soup garnished with lump crab, followed by Shrimp Malacca over rice. The latter was a recipe from Maurice Moore-Betty, the dapper Irish-born cookbook author and teacher who was a great friend of James Beard, and it turned out to be, I realize now, Shrimp Creole with a generous dose of curry powder. Häagen-Dazs had just reached the freezer case of our local grocery store, which was cause for great excitement, so for dessert we had lemon sorbet with Pepperidge Farm Bordeaux cookies, then the height of sophistication (and still, let's face it, pretty damn delicious). There was plenty of white wine to drink and the whole evening turned out to be a big success—despite the fact that it was very likely around 90 degrees well after the sun had gone down.

That long-ago dinner turned out to be a useful blueprint. These days, I do most of my entertaining in New Orleans, where it's at least as hot as the Delta and where shellfish is so abundant it would be crazy not to serve it all the time. No matter what the temperature, I rarely start a party without passing some incarnation of fried oysters as hors d'oeuvres. For years, I plopped them on buttered and toasted slices of baguette with a dab of homemade tartar sauce. I still do, and they are delicious, but once I added Jason Epstein's fried oysters in lettuce boats to my repertoire, people literally started chasing down the trays as they went by.

Not only are the oysters that good, they are extraordinarily easy to make. First, slice romaine lettuce hearts in strips about two inches long—just long enough to hold an oyster. Next, take some plain old Hellman's mayonnaise and stir in some lemon juice, cayenne pepper, and chopped chives. Put a small dollop of the mayo in the "vees" of the lettuce pieces, fry the oysters in corn flour (Zatarain's unseasoned Fish-Fri is perfect) until crisp and golden brown, sprinkle with salt, and plop them on top of the mayo. The juxtaposition of the hot crispy oyster with the cold lettuce and mayo is reminiscent of a BLT. In fact, I've had chef friends gild the lily by adding crumbled bacon to the mayonnaise. Don't do it. And don't make home-made mayo—in this case the doctored Hellman's is better.

I still occasionally make the soup I made for Alexis—the cool pale green of the cucumber and avocado seems to somehow take the edge off the heat. But if you are feeling especially flush, the same effect can be created with a mound of jumbo lump crab on Boston lettuce leaves topped with a generous spoonful of green goddess dressing. That too, was inspired by a friend—in this case Suzanne Rheinstein, the gifted New Orleans–born interior designer and fabulous hostess, who served it at a Southern dinner in my honor. The colors—creamy, herby celadon atop a snowy mound—are as stunning as the taste.

For a main course, Shrimp Malacca remains a winner. You can make the sauce well ahead of time and the curry is an inspired touch. It is also helpful in the hot weather. The nineteenth-century English believed that heat slowed down the digestive system and the curry powders they learned to make from the Indians worked as a stimulant.

To end the meal, "cold" and "lemon" remain my warm-weather bywords. I love the soufflé below but lemon sorbet or ice cream would also be swell, accompanied by crispy cookies. You could do worse than hauling out the bag of Bordeaux, but you could also take another leaf from Suzanne's book and make chocolate chip cookies without the chips. They are genius. So are the Pimm's Royales (see page 108) that would be the perfect cocktail to start.

GREEN GODDESS DRESSING

(*Yield: About 2 cups*)

1 bunch green onions, roughly chopped with some of the
    green tops

1 garlic clove, crushed

⅓ cup parsley, roughly chopped

2 tablespoons tarragon leaves, roughly chopped

3 tablespoons chives, roughly chopped

1 cup mayonnaise, homemade or Hellman's

3 tablespoons lemon juice, or more to taste

3 tablespoons anchovy paste

½ cup sour cream

Salt and freshly ground black pepper

Mix all ingredients except sour cream and salt and pepper in food processor until green onions and herbs are finely chopped and the mixture is well blended. Place mixture in mixing bowl and fold in sour cream. Add salt and pepper and check for seasoning.

SHRIMP MALACCA

(*Yield: 8 servings*)

⅓ cup vegetable or canola oil

2 medium yellow onions, finely diced

1 large green pepper, seeded, cored, and finely diced

2 ribs celery, peeled and diced (about ½ cup)

One 16-ounce can peeled Italian plum tomatoes

1 cup tomato puree

Generous pinch cayenne pepper

Generous pinch dried basil

2 garlic cloves, mashed with 1 teaspoon of coarse salt

2 bay leaves

Salt

Freshly ground black pepper

2 tablespoons curry powder

3 pounds medium shrimp, peeled and deveined

Heat the oil in a large heavy saucepan. Add onions, green
pepper, and celery, and cook until soft, stirring occasionally.

Add tomatoes, tomato puree, cayenne, basil, garlic,
bay leaves, and salt and pepper to taste. Bring to a boil and
add curry powder. Lower the heat and simmer the mixture,
covered, for about 25 minutes. If the sauce seems too thick,
thin it with a little seafood stock or water. Add the shrimp and

simmer about 10 minutes, or until just cooked through. Serve with rice.

COLD LEMON SOUFFLÉ

(*Yield: 6 to 8 servings*)

3 eggs, separated, plus 1 extra egg white

1 cup sugar

½ cup water

1 tablespoon gelatin

⅓ cup lemon juice

Grated rind of 2 lemons

1 teaspoon vanilla

2 cups heavy cream

Prepare a soufflé dish with an upstanding collar of folded wax paper (you'll want to fold it into several layers) high enough to come halfway up again over the top of the dish. Brush the paper with vegetable oil (or spray with unflavored and unscented Pam) and tie securely around the dish.

Beat egg yolks with sugar (preferably with an electric mixer) until the mixture is pale, thick, and fluffy.

Put the water in a small bowl, sprinkle in gelatin, and stir. Put the bowl over a pan of simmering water until gelatin has dissolved completely. Add a couple of tablespoons of the egg mixture to the gelatin and then carefully mix the two together. Add lemon juice, rind, and vanilla, and mix well.

Beat the 4 egg whites until stiff and fold ⅓ into egg mixture, then fold in the rest. Beat 1½ cups of the whipped cream until soft peaks form and fold it in.

Pour into soufflé dish and chill for at least 3 hours. Meanwhile, whip the rest of the cream. When ready to serve, peel off wax paper collar and decorate with rosettes of the whipped cream. Candied lemon peel looks pretty on top as well, or you could gently press chopped toasted almonds around the sides.

NOTE: The preparation here is the most dramatic way to present the soufflé, but serving it from a nice glass bowl is fine.

· 24 ·

Weddings, Royal
and Otherwise

If the rich are different from you and me, then the British royals definitely are. Queen Elizabeth is not only the Head of State of the United Kingdom and fifteen other Commonwealth realms, she has a personal net worth estimated at $500 million, she gets an annual stipend of $12.5 million, and has the use of real estate valued at $15 billion. You would think, then, that the 2011 wedding of her grandson Prince William and Kate Middleton would have been an extravaganza far, far different that the nuptial events of us mere mortals. But based on my close attention to the official royal wedding Web site before the event, as well as to the reams of news coverage during and after, it appeared to me that the whole thing was sort of, well, normal. To borrow yet another overused literary reference, it seems that like all happy families, most weddings—and the dilemmas they present—are very much alike.

First, let's examine the guest list. The royal family, like

most families with a divorce or two in the mix (which would include a huge majority of American families, since more than 50 percent of everyone on this side of the pond who gets married also gets divorced), is saddled with some former in-laws with whom there is some seriously bad blood. In this case, the pesky in-laws were the family of Princess Diana, who normally would have been seated on the groom's side. But in a brilliant move that we should all use henceforth as a model, they were safely seated across the vast Westminster Abbey aisle with the family of the bride instead. Then, there were the required invitees. Among the many who could not be snubbed were the governors general who represent the Queen in Commonwealth realms outside the U.K., a group that includes the Right Honorable Sir Anand Satyanand of New Zealand, for example, but not, of course, our own president. Other must-have guests were members of various religious organizations, representatives of William's charities, and members of the diplomatic corps—a situation not all that dissimilar to Elizabeth Cordes's wedding to which she was forced to invite every single customer of the Bank of Leland, Mississippi, where her father served as president. Likewise, just before I canceled my own wedding of 1,000-plus guests, invitations had already been addressed to the entire congregation of the local First Presbyterian Church, most of my father's political and business colleagues, and all of the bridesmaids and groomsmen from my parents' own nuptials. Considering the fact that the Windsors have a few more responsibilities, their guest list of a mere 1,800 seems comparatively modest.

Despite the huge number, Elizabeth's nighttime event was really beautiful and really, really fun, featuring a lavish cocktail supper and a great dance band. Unfortunately for her, she missed most of it—by the time she and her husband finished greeting the masses in the receiving line, it was almost ten P.M. and time to head off to the airport and their honeymoon. Again, I have to say that the royals have come up with an ingenious solution to the receiving line dilemma. Since William and Kate's ceremony took place in the morning, they held a noontime reception featuring champagne and canapés. Not only is this elegant combination one of my favorites (when I finally did get married, the champagne was Churchill's favorite, Pol Roger, and the canapés included both cucumber and watercress sandwiches and blini with ossetra), it allowed the new couple to get all the official greeting and hobnobbing out of the way before attending a more intimate dinner dance with real friends and family on the same evening.

After the dinner dance, Prince Harry took over some rooms at Buckingham Palace for a late-night disco party. Again, I am reminded of Elizabeth's reception, which, despite the departure of the bride and groom, continued with great gusto into the not-so-wee hours of the following morning and cranked up again at an impromptu lunch, which in turn stretched into the evening. By that time, we'd run out of food and Elizabeth's sister McGee and I were dispatched to the Wendy's drive-through to pick up a few hundred dollars' worth of burgers and baked potatoes for the grateful hangers-on, who were in need of restorative doses of grease and potassium, respectively. I don't know what Harry featured on his own menu, but ours was not a bad combo to emulate. In fact, Elizabeth took it up a notch when she served late-night hamburger sliders and cones of fries at her eldest daughter's debutante party.

Other similarities between the royals and commoners abound. In addition to the traditional tiered wedding cake, William requested his favorite chocolate biscuit cake, which sounds a lot like our typically chocolate grooms' cakes (though his was, thankfully, not in the shape of an armadillo, a particularly obnoxious Southern custom my friend Bobby Harling immortalized in his movie *Steel Magnolias*). The groom's cakes at my own wedding were elegant petit fours iced in chocolate with my husband's initials in white, and the wedding cake itself was a white cake flavored with almond, a simple but delicious choice we finally hit on after I made at least half a dozen more complicated samples in my mother's kitchen, including a Lady Baltimore Cake and another with lemon curd layers.

The great thing about getting married at forty-two is that pretty much all the choices are your own, including the menu, and you are not obligated to ask a thousand of your family's closest friends. We served our 100-plus guests the aforementioned canapés, along with an elegant *jambon persille* and Julia Child's chicken mousse with foie gras. There was rare tenderloin and lots of shrimp and crabmeat and cold asparagus and celery root remoulade. It's a menu I seem to come back to in some form or another with regard to nuptial celebrations. For my friend M. T.'s rehearsal dinner (held at my parents' house a few months after my own wedding there) we made daube glacé and served it with asparagus vinaigrette and a huge platter featuring shrimp in a mustardy Creole remoulade sauce alongside celery root in a classic white one. There was no receiving line at either event and, unlike poor Elizabeth and her husband, we stayed—and stayed—to enjoy our own afterparties.

JAMBON PERSILLE OR PARSLEYED HAM IN ASPIC

(*Yield: 10 appetizer servings*)

1 bottle dry white Burgundy

¾ cup chicken stock

4 shallots

2 garlic cloves

2 bay leaves

3 sprigs tarragon

1 teaspoon black peppercorns

1 large bunch curly parsley

One 2-pound piece of cooked ham

2 tablespoons Knox gelatin

Salt and freshly ground white pepper

Combine wine, roughly half the stock, shallots, garlic, bay leaves, tarragon, and peppercorns in saucepan. Cover, bring to boil, and reduce to simmer. Strip parsley leaves from stems and add stems to simmering wine mixture. Let simmer for 30 minutes. Wash and dry parsley leaves, chop them, and place them in small bowl. Pour ¼ cup of boiling water over leaves to set the color and leave to cool. Divide ham into uneven chunks, discarding fat and any sinew. (The finished aspic looks best if the ham is pulled apart into big slivers with fingers rather than cutting into cubes with knife.)

Pour remaining stock into medium bowl, sprinkle gelatin on top, and leave it until spongy, about 5 minutes. Strain wine mixture into measuring cup—there should be about 3 cups, but if not, add a little water. Bring wine mixture just back to boil and pour it over gelatin. Let stand for a minute, then stir to melt the gelatin. Taste aspic, season with salt and pepper (remember, the ham is already salty), and leave to cool until tepid. Aspic will thicken quite suddenly when cool, so don't chill it.

To mold the ham, add shallow layer of aspic to 2-quart glass bowl or terrine mold and chill in refrigerator or over ice water until set. Mix ham with parsley (along with its liquid) in large bowl. Add remaining tepid aspic, mix well, and transfer to mold. Press the pieces of ham well below the surface of the aspic and make sure no air bubbles are trapped beneath the ham. Cover the mold and chill it until set, at least 6 hours. It keeps well for up to a week, but once cut open should be eaten within a day or two.

To serve, dip the mold in hot water for 15 to 30 seconds to loosen the aspic. Run a knife around the edge, unmold the ham onto a platter, and cut it in wedges or slices.

CELERY ROOT REMOULADE

(*Yield: 6 servings*)

1 pound celery root

Juice of 1 fresh lemon

1 cup (approximately) remoulade sauce (recipe below)

Salt

Freshly ground white pepper

Minced parsley

Peel the celery root and cut out any deep brown grooves. Cut into workable pieces and grate coarsely using a hand grater or food processor. Place into a bowl of cold water with the lemon juice. Allow to sit for 10 minutes. Drain and place in a towel and squeeze out the excess moisture. Toss with 1 cup remoulade, adding more as needed but be careful not to overdress so that the sweet, earthy flavor of the celery root is not masked. Add salt and pepper if needed, and sprinkle with parsley.

Remoulade Sauce

(*Yield: About 1¼ cups*)

1 large egg

1 tablespoon Dijon mustard

1 teaspoon rinsed capers

1 teaspoon chopped cornichons

1 anchovy, rinsed and chopped

1 tablespoon each, chopped fresh chervil, tarragon, parsley, and chives

Juice of 1 lemon

1 tablespoon champagne vinegar

1 cup vegetable oil

2 tablespoons olive oil

Salt and freshly ground white pepper

Place all the ingredients except the oils and salt and pepper in the work bowl of a food processor, fitted with the steel blade. Blend until very frothy then slowly drizzle the oils (while the machine is still running) in a thin stream until uniform and well blended. Stop and taste, adjust seasonings with salt and white pepper. Remove and store covered in the refrigerator until needed.

· 25 ·

A Pilgrim's Progress

The first Thanksgiving dinner I cooked on my own, I was a junior in college and living off Washington's Dupont Circle in a narrow, second-floor walk-up apartment with exposed brick walls, a boat shower from Hammacher-Schlemmer in the minuscule (black!) bathroom, and a kitchen with a single oven, a freestanding sink, and no counters. Any meal more elaborate than about two dishes was always a major undertaking—mainly because chopping meant kneeling on the floor over a cutting board and stirring meant sitting with a bowl anchored between my knees.

It didn't matter. I loved that apartment and I loved cooking for a motley group of friends that included (on that particular day): a male and a female former roommate, a childhood friend I hadn't seen in fifteen years, and a *New York Times* photographer from my hometown, as well as his medical student wife. Determined to impress, I dutifully followed the directions in my battered *Joy of Cooking* and covered the turkey's breast in cheesecloth soaked in melted butter and vegetable oil. I made a savory sweet potato gratin from a recipe I found in *Gourmet,* the yummy oyster dressing from *Joy,* and that ubiquitous green bean casserole topped with Durkee's fried onions, which might be a tiny bit gross and definitely a little tacky, but also really tasty.

We gathered in my living room around my mother's old kitchen table, drank a lot of cheap red wine, pulled out pretty much every LP I owned, and carried on well into the night. In an ancient scrapbook somewhere, there are pictures of us dancing. It remains one of the most memorable Thanksgivings I've ever had, not least, I'm certain, because it was the first I'd done one on my own and I dared to veer off the family script. There were no oranges stuffed with overly sweetened sweet potatoes and topped with marshmallows, a dish de rigueur at the house I grew up in and my grandmother's before that, but which I cannot abide. I finally got to have the bean casserole that graced the table of my friends with slightly less tasteful mothers; the dressing was made of French bread as opposed to cornbread (horrors!), and the pie was chess rather than pecan.

Since then, I've cooked at least twenty more Thanksgiving meals. I've brined turkeys, deep-fried turkeys, sought out hard-to-find heritage breeds, and the best butchers from whom to order a Turducken. I've broken down and stuffed the dread oranges with sweet potatoes (sweetened only with the juice from the oranges and enlivened with a healthy dose of brandy), albeit with no marshmallows (buttered bread crumbs with orange zest and finely chopped pecans makes a far less cloying topping), and discovered the significant pleasures of Brussels sprouts. I've copied the delicious purees of my friend

Jason Epstein (his cauliflower with curry and his rutabaga and apple with a tiny bit of maple syrup are always huge hits), and made like the Cajuns and forgone bread dressing in favor of dirty rice and mirlitons stuffed with crab and shrimp. For a stretch of almost ten years I freed myself from Thanksgiving altogether by having a grand time in London instead.

But after a while, I missed it: the planning, the camaraderie, even the rising at dawn to start the prep. And then, of course, there's the significance of the day itself. On the first Thanksgiving after Katrina, one of the few pieces of furniture in our halfway-renovated house was a gift from my father, an enormous dining room table that seats twenty-four. The storm was less than three months behind us; those of us living full-time in the still sparsely populated city felt like pioneers and I was determined to fill my new table with all the stray pilgrims I knew. After all the guests had arrived, the kitchen sink overflowed and flooded the kitchen (my idiot plumber had forgotten to replace the outgoing pipe with one that was, say, wider than a quarter-inch, the width of the heavily corroded old one), and further catastrophe struck when my mother drained the tub in the guest bathroom (the same idiot did not connect the drain to a pipe of any kind, so that all the water poured straight through the ceiling). None of it mattered—we formed a tipsy mop brigade and then sat down and gave thanks to our extraordinary luck and the blessing not only of being together, but of being alive.

Since then, I wouldn't dream of forgoing Thanksgiving. Last year, sixteen of us sat at a long table outside and ate a feast as close as we could get to the real pilgrims' first one, which as it turns out, probably didn't feature a turkey. In fact, it didn't have much of anything we now equate with the Thanksgiving table. There was no stuffing (the dearth of flour meant there was no bread to make it with), no rolls (ditto), no potatoes (most Europeans still thought they were poisonous), no pumpkin pie (pumpkin and winter squash were served boiled), not even any cranberries (they'd yet to be introduced). We know for sure that Governor William Bradford sent "four men fowling" after wild geese and ducks. They may or may not have returned with a turkey or two as well, and possibly a swan, but they definitely augmented their bounty by copious amounts of venison (Bradford was presented with at least five deer) and the seafood that was abundant on the coast. There was corn, of course, and foraged wild mushrooms, and the watercress that grew on creek banks.

For our own Plymouth-style celebration, we grilled oysters on the half shell alongside venison sausages and duck sausages. We roasted a duck and a wild turkey (just in case), made shrimp and crab dressing and cornbread dressing with chanterelles. We made corn pudding with caramelized leeks and finished up with a watercress salad with toasted pecans. It was a glorious day and now a tradition requiring that all participants wear feathered headdresses or Pilgrim hats. Another—longstanding—tradition is the pitcher of icy (and eye-opening) Red Roosters that Elizabeth Cordes always brings over to kick-start the festivities.

The menu will keep changing, as always. Elizabeth will likely bring the sweet potato-stuffed oranges that her children still insist on, while I'll make some version of that long-ago sweet potato gratin and the cranberry conserve I have to have with my turkey. Always there are oysters, sometimes in the French bread dressing of my college feast, sometimes in a red rice and andouille dressing inspired by Scott Peacock.

And then, of course, there's pie—Jason's pear tarte Tatin (see page 59) and some version of pecan or chess or both. In November there are usually so many key limes falling off my trees, I should really add a classic key lime pie to the mix. It may not be in keeping with the traditions of the season, but seriously, who likes pumpkin pie?

RED ROOSTER
(*Yield: 8 to 10 drinks*)

1½ quarts cranberry juice cocktail

One 6-ounce can frozen orange juice concentrate

2 cups vodka

Lime slices, for garnish

Mix juices and vodka well and put in a Tupperware bowl with a lid or a wide-mouth pitcher with a screw top. Freeze. The vodka will keep the mixture from freezing hard. When ready to serve, transfer to a pitcher and stir. It should have the consistency of a slushy. Garnish each glass with a lime slice.

CRANBERRY CONSERVE

(*Yield: About 8 cups*)

Five unpeeled oranges, halved and sliced

1 cup apple juice

1½ cups fresh pineapple, cut into half-inch chunks

Three 12–ounce bags cranberries

2 cups honey (orange blossom is especially nice in this recipe)

1 cup turbinado sugar

½ cup freshly squeezed lemon juice

1½ teaspoons ground cinnamon

2 teaspoons whole cloves

1 tablespoon freshly grated ginger

Place orange slices in heavy-bottomed pot, large enough to hold cranberries. Add apple juice and simmer for about 10 minutes.

Add remaining ingredients and bring to a boil. Reduce heat and simmer, stirring often until thick, about 35 minutes.

Ladle into clean jars. The conserve will keep, tightly covered, in the refrigerator for up to 3 weeks.

OYSTER RED RICE DRESSING

(*Yield: 8 to 10 servings*)

6 tablespoons butter

2 cups shucked, drained oysters, liquor reserved

Salt and freshly ground black pepper

1½ pounds andouille sausage

6 tablespoons bacon fat

1 cup chopped onion

½ cup chopped green bell pepper

2 teaspoons dried thyme

½ teaspoon cayenne pepper

2 tablespoons minced garlic

2 tablespoons tomato paste

2½ cups canned whole peeled tomatoes, roughly chopped

1 cup chicken stock

2 cups long-grain rice

1 bunch thinly sliced green onions, including a bit of pale
green tops

Preheat the oven to 325 degrees.

Melt 4 tablespoons of the butter in a large sauté pan over
medium low heat until foaming. Add the oysters, seasoning
lightly with salt and black pepper, and sauté quickly, until the

edges just begin to curl, about a minute. Drain over a bowl to collect juices and add them to the reserved oyster liquor.

Pour about ½ inch of water into a heavy skillet, add the sausage, and cook over low heat, uncovered, about 10 minutes, until the water has cooked off. When the sausage has cooled, cut in thin slices and then cut in half again. Heat the bacon fat in the same skillet and add the onion. Cook for about 8 minutes, until onion is translucent, and add bell pepper, thyme, cayenne, and garlic. Cook, stirring occasionally, for another 10 minutes. Add salt and pepper to taste, tomato paste, and tomatoes, and continue to cook for about 3 minutes.

Measure the oyster liquor and add enough stock to make 2½ cups. Add to the vegetables, cover, and simmer gently, stirring often, for about 15 minutes.

Melt the remaining 2 tablespoons of butter in a large, heavy pot or Dutch oven. Add the rice and cook over medium heat for 2 minutes, stirring constantly until grains are well-coated. Add the sausage and the tomato mixture. Stir and cover tightly. Cook over low to medium-low heat for about 20 minutes, until rice is tender. Toss in the oysters and green onions and taste for seasoning. Spoon into a buttered casserole dish and bake for 30 minutes.

SAVORY SWEET POTATO GRATIN

(*Yield: 6 to 8 servings*)

3 to 3½ pounds sweet potatoes

2 tablespoons butter

1 small yellow onion, diced

3 garlic cloves, minced

5 bay leaves (fresh, preferably)

1 leafy branch thyme

2 cups cream

¼ cup dry white wine

½ to 1 cup chicken stock

Salt and freshly ground black pepper

1 cup grated Gruyère cheese

1 cup grated Parmesan

Peel potatoes and slice into thin rounds, preferably with a mandoline or with a Cuisinart slicing attachment. Set aside and preheat the oven to 375 degrees. Butter a 9×13-inch baking dish.

Melt 1 tablespoon of the butter in a medium saucepan over medium heat and add onions. Stir occasionally for about 5 minutes, until onions are translucent. Lower heat, add garlic, and cook, stirring constantly, for a minute or two more.

Add bay leaves, thyme branch, and white wine, and increase heat to medium-high. Reduce until most of the wine has been cooked out. Add cream and return the mixture to a simmer. Lower heat and maintain the mixture at a simmer until it is reduced to 1½ cups, which may take as long as an hour.

Remove thyme branch and bay leaves (if using dried) from reduced cream. Transfer to a blender and blend for about a minute. Strain through mesh strainer into a mixing cup, and stir in ½ cup of the chicken stock. Spread ½ cup of the mixture evenly over bottom of baking dish and arrange half of the sweet potato slices on top in slightly overlapping rows. Season with salt and pepper and sprinkle with half of both cheeses and then another ½ cup of the cream. Cover with remaining potato slices, sprinkle again with salt and pepper, and add the remaining cream and cheese.

Cover tightly with foil and bake for 40 minutes. Remove foil and drizzle with the remaining chicken stock if the gratin seems dry. Return gratin to the oven and bake for another 20 minutes, until cheese is crisp and golden on top.

RUM PECAN PIE

(*Yield: 8 servings*)

1 partially baked 9-inch pie shell (see below)

5 tablespoons butter

1¼ cups pecan halves

1 teaspoon salt

4 eggs

1½ cups packed light brown sugar

1 teaspoon vanilla extract

3 tablespoons dark rum, preferably Barbancourt

Preheat the oven to 375 degrees.

Melt 1 tablespoon of the butter in a medium-sized saucepan over low heat. Toss pecans in the pan and sprinkle with the salt. Spread in a single layer on a cookie sheet and place in preheated oven. After 5 minutes, stir the nuts, and, watching carefully, bake for another 5 minutes, until they have just begun to color. Let cool.

Melt remaining 4 tablespoons butter over low heat in a saucepan and set aside to cool. Meanwhile, break eggs into mixing bowl and beat until smooth. Add sugar and stir until sugar is dissolved. Stir in the butter, vanilla, and rum until smooth. Fold in pecans and pour into the prepared shell.

Bake for 10 minutes. Reduce the heat to 325 degrees and bake until filling is set, about 30 minutes.

Serve warm, if possible, with lightly whipped cream (add 3 tablespoons sugar and 1 teaspoon each of vanilla and rum for each cup of heavy cream) or vanilla ice cream.

FOR THE PARTIALLY BAKED PIE SHELL

1 cup all-purpose flour

¼ teaspoon salt

3 tablespoons butter, cut into ¼ -inch chunks

2 tablespoons lard, cut into small chunks (vegetable short-
    ening or more butter may be substituted)
About ¼ cup ice water

Place flour and salt in a food processor fitted with a steel blade
that has been chilled in the freezer. Pulse it a few times to sift
flour, then add butter and lard. Pulse the machine until the
flour looks like coarse meal. (You can do this by hand by
whisking the flour and then cutting in the butter and lard with
a fork or pastry blender.)

Add ⅛ cup cold water and pulse (or mix by hand
with fork). Pulse and add more water until mixture just
begins holding together and is no longer sticky or wet.
Quickly gather it into a ball, lightly dust with flour,
wrap well with plastic wrap, and flatten it into a half-inch
disk. Refrigerate for at least 20 minutes before rolling it
out.

Roll out dough on a lightly floured surface until you have
a circle of 13½ inches in diameter; gently fold in half and then
in half again. Put the point at the midpoint of the pie plate,
carefully unfold, and gently press into the edges of the plate.
The pastry should extend ½ inch all around the lip of the
plate. Trim (and save) any messy excess and crimp the edge
decoratively. (My friend, the brilliant food historian and stylist
Rick Ellis, makes a bit of extra dough and rims the pie in
individual dough "leaves" that he has "veined" with a knife.)
Lightly butter a piece of foil, drape it over the pie plate buttered side down so that it covers the edges, and press it very
lightly into the contours of the pie shell. Pour in 1½ cups dried
beans or rice. Bake 15 minutes, remove from oven, and care-

fully lift out foil and beans. Prick bottom with fork and repair any cracks with reserved trimmings. Return to oven for 10 to 15 more minutes, until it is beginning to color and the bottom looks dry.

NOTE: The trick to a good pecan pie is to salt, butter, and toast the pecans first. You may of course use bourbon with this recipe, preferably a good small-batch brand.

· 26 ·

Visions of Sugarplums

Several years ago I went on a wishful shopping spree and ended up with a closet full of fabulous frocks and shoes and evening bags, all perfect for a holiday party. The only problem was that nobody was having one—or at least not the kind that demanded a black velvet YSL gown, a navy silk Oscar de la Renta cocktail dress, or a pair of purple satin Manolo Blahnik pumps. So I wrote a piece in *Vogue* bemoaning the lack of truly festive holiday entertaining and I got a boatload of letters back from people who were equally starved.

I said that what I really wanted for Christmas was a return to the glam parties of my youth. Not to an office Christmas party like in the movies, where everybody gets drunk and wears funny hats and somebody invariably gets caught with somebody else on top of the Xerox machine. Nor did I mean a real-life office party, one of those boring corporate affairs usually held in restaurants where they start setting tables for real customers at eight o'clock so that everybody has to clear out. (And the ones that drag on are even worse, full of all that obligatory camaraderie—there's no romance, no glamour, not even the hint of surprise.) What I had hoped for that year, and pretty much every year since, was a real old-fashioned holiday party, one that's big and lavish and even a little magical, where all the guests look beautiful and behave accordingly—a party like the one in the opening scene of *The Nutcracker* (my favorite version is Mikhail Baryshnikov's, because the wife gets a diamond necklace just before the guests arrive).

When I was nine, my mother had three of these parties back-to-back, with at least a hundred people each, and I got to wear the blue velvet dress with the white lace collar I wore in my aunt's wedding as I took the coats at the door. A sexy Englishman I'd never seen before tipped me with a two-dollar bill, which I kept for years as a souvenir, a link not only to this unspeakably handsome man but also to the soigné night in which I had played a tiny part. My mother had a different outfit for each party, and my favorite was a white silk crepe pantsuit, with narrow pants and a short-sleeved tunic that had a sort of Greek key neckline adorned with hunky glass sapphires, emeralds, and rubies. It was very Versace and very chic and I would wear it now myself, but for the fact that about two minutes before the guests arrived my little brother threw a cup of Welch's grape juice from his high chair onto my mother's snow-white front, and she had to change into the red-and-gold plaid hostess skirt and red satin blouse she'd worn the night before.

I will never forget the preparations that went into those parties, the garland everywhere and the enormous tree with what seemed like hundreds of strings of tiny white lights and the dozens and dozens of votive candles that had to be lit with long matches at the very last minute. There were bartenders in white jackets and hordes of people in the kitchen buttering homemade rolls and making horseradish sauce for the tenderloin, adding sherry to the Seafood Newburg. And the guests made an effort, too—they looked different, better, far more glamorous than they did at any other time in the year. The ladies wore hairpieces or even tinsel in their hair, and dark eye makeup and big earrings (this was the sixties); the men wore red vests and holly pants and ties with tiny Christmas trees. They laughed more and talked faster. Their cheeks were flushed and their senses heightened. Turned on by the brisk weather, or the pine scent, or the booze, or the sheer built-in anticipation of the season, they all acted as if they knew something exciting and wonderful was going to happen before the evening ended—they just didn't know what it was yet. New Year's parties are always awful because they are about pressure (to have fun, to get drunk, to be kissed); at their best, Christmas parties are about possibility. School's out and work's over and people's houses aren't their houses anymore—the furniture's all rearranged to make room for the Christmas tree; angels fly from the ceiling. They've become sets, and the thing about sets is that whatever happens inside them is fantasy.

In these trying times, all of us are overdue for a touch of fantasy, not to mention possibility. We owe it to ourselves to do more than just get through with work and finish shopping and frantically send FedEx packages. I do not want to race to a finish line that involves sweaters and sweatpants and Netflix. I'm ready for some sugarplums to be dancing in my head; I want my pulse to quicken as I mount someone's front steps and push open a door to discover something intimate and grand at the same time. I want to see people I love and people I'll want to. And I want to dress up, a lot. One year for the annual holiday bash her parents used to throw, my friend M. T. bought a red taffeta gown with a full skirt and a tight bodice marked by a breathtakingly low ruffled neckline. Her grandmother took one look at it and told her that people would talk and she said, "Oh, Nana, if they only would." Exactly.

The first clothes I wore to holiday parties were the ones I got for Christmas. We always had lots of people over on Christmas night, and my earliest ensembles at these events included an Indian-chief costume with full headdress from FAO Schwarz and a gypsy dress with a black velvet sequined bodice and a multicolored striped satin skirt. The other girls wore red or green velvet dresses and the boys wore matching jumpers or pants with white oxfords, and we would drink sparkling Catawba grape juice and pretend it was champagne, and set off Roman candles on the front porch, and eat dressing balls and bourbon balls, and spy on the adults, which we could not wait to be.

Since our house was the venue for Christmas, the McGees threw an enormous party on Christmas Eve. The first year I didn't have to go upstairs and eat cookies and drink punch with the children was a major milestone in my life. Downstairs, the drinks were served in silver julep cups and there were all kinds of things in chafing dishes to eat with toast points, and red velvet cake and caramel cakes, and women with long legs and long necks sitting on the stairs, looking up with bright eyes and naughty smiles at the men they were talking to. One year at one of these parties I kissed a man on the roof of the house (it was Victorian, and you could walk right out the upstairs dormer windows and find a level place to stand); another year a man got locked in the bathroom (adorned with greenery and red and white bunting and scented Christmas candles) and there was so much noise that nobody heard him, so he called his babysitter at home and told her to call back and tell whoever answered the phone to come and find him. It took the babysitter three tries to find anybody who cared enough to stop what they were doing long enough to get him out.

A few years later at one of my parents' shindigs, an old beau of mine—uninvited—walked through the front door at midnight, sat down, and started playing the piano. The next thing I knew someone had woken up my neighbor to get a guitar, and somebody else found a tambourine, and we stuck holly in our hair and drank gin and danced and made up song lyrics about, of all things, the fall of the Ceauşescus and Czechoslovakia's Velvet Revolution. (This, obviously, was in 1989; one of the few lines I still recall is "Dubček is a redneck.") I remember that I had on a very short iridescent green velvet dress and earrings so long they grazed my shoulders, and that my fiancé at the time had gone to bed extremely early. It was raining so hard when it was finally time to go that everybody's cars got stuck in the front yard. So we ate breakfast and sang some more instead.

That was a long time ago and, unfortunately, one of the last great Christmas parties I've been to. Recently, I asked a friend of mine how long it had been since she'd been to a great one and she said never. I feel like I owe it to her and to me and to everybody else I know to step in and take up the banner once carried by my mother and all her friends. Their parties always included at least one chafing dish filled with the aforementioned Seafood Newburg and another with Spinach Madeleine (see page 16). My mother served tenderloin on yeast rolls with horseradish sauce, and paper-thin slices of the country ham my grandmother sent from Tennessee on biscuits or more rolls with hot mustard. I'm going to do all that and more, including passing plenty of hors d'oeuvres and canapés and making at least one of the holiday punches on pages 132 and 133. With any luck someone will end up smooching on the roof.

JULIA CHILD'S ROQUEFORT CHEESE BALLS

(Yield: About 24 balls)

½ pound Roquefort or other good blue cheese

4 to 6 tablespoons softened butter

1½ tablespoons minced chives

1 tablespoon finely minced celery

Pinch of cayenne pepper

⅛ teaspoon freshly ground black pepper

Salt, if needed

2 teaspoons cognac (you may substitute 1 teaspoon Worcestershire sauce)

½ cup fine, stale, white bread crumbs

2 tablespoons very finely minced parsley

Crush the cheese in a bowl with 4 tablespoons of the butter and work it into a smooth paste. Beat in the chives, celery, seasonings, and cognac. If mixture is very stiff, beat in more butter by fractions. Check seasoning carefully, adding salt if necessary. Roll into balls about ½ inch in diameter.

Toss bread crumbs and parsley in a bowl and turn out onto a plate. Roll the cheese balls in the mixture so they are well covered. Chill.

WATERMELON PICKLE
HORS D'OEUVRES
(*Yield: About 20 pieces*)

One (10-ounce) jar Haddon House Sweet Pickled
    Watermelon Rind

10 pieces bacon, cut in half

Preheat oven to 375 degrees. Drain watermelon. Roll bacon around each piece and secure with a toothpick. Place on ungreased cookie sheet and bake until bacon is well browned, about 20 minutes.

NOTE: This is the world's easiest hors d'oeuvre and people go crazy for it. For the bacon, use plain old Oscar Mayer or Bryan or a similar brand—this doesn't work with thick-cut bacon and you don't need applewood smoked or anything else remotely fancy. For the pickles, if

I'm eating them plain, I like a less sweet (read homemade) watermelon pickle. But for this recipe, the syrup of the Haddon House pickle is the perfect foil for the salty bacon, and the result is a caramelized piece of perfection.

SEAFOOD NEWBURG

(*Yield: About 8 to 10 cups*)

1½ sticks butter

4 tablespoons minced shallots

5 cups cooked shellfish, cut into ½-inch pieces

1 cup sherry or Madeira

3 teaspoons salt

½ teaspoon white pepper

Cayenne pepper

4 tablespoons of flour

3 cups heavy cream

3 egg yolks

1 tablespoon lemon juice

2 cups sliced button mushrooms, sautéed in butter and seasoned with salt and white pepper

1½ teaspoons paprika

In a large saucepan, melt 1 stick of the butter, add shallots, and cook for 1 to 2 minutes over low heat, until just softened. Add shellfish and wine and bring to a simmer. Raise heat slightly, and cook until liquid has almost completely boiled away. Season with salt, white pepper, and a pinch of cayenne, and set aside.

In a large saucepan, melt the remaining half stick of butter, sprinkle in the flour, whisking constantly, and cook slowly for 2 or 3 minutes. Do not allow to color. Remove from heat. Bring 2 cups cream to a boil and stir it into the flour mixture. Bring mixture back to a boil and cook, stirring, for 1 minute.

Beat egg yolks and remaining cup of cream in a bowl. Remove sauce from heat and beat it into the bowl in ¼-cup increments. Return to saucepan and boil, stirring, for 1 minute. It should be pretty thick.

Stir in lemon juice and paprika. Fold in mushrooms and seafood and check seasoning.

For cocktail parties, serve in a chafing dish with toast points (triangles of Pepperidge Farm or similarly good white bread, crusts off, and baked in a 250-degree oven until completely dry but not brown). For a main course, serve over rice or puff pastry shells.

NOTE: I usually use a combination of shrimp and crabmeat because that's easiest to put my hands on where I live, but lobster is wonderful in it, of course, as are scallops. Mix and match or use all four. Some people like a bit of nutmeg and I usually add a bit of cognac or Worcestershire in the end, and maybe a touch more sherry too. As always, the trick is to taste. It should be rich in flavor and luxurious in texture.

BOURBON BALLS

(*Yield: About 36 balls*)

One 12-ounce box Nilla wafers, pulverized to a fine crumb
   in a food processor

2 tablespoons cocoa powder

1 cup powdered sugar, plus more for rolling

1 cup finely chopped pecans

2 tablespoons light corn syrup

½ cup bourbon

Combine all ingredients in a large mixing bowl and mix well.
Form into 1-inch balls and roll in powdered sugar. Stored in an
airtight container and refrigerated, the balls will keep for up to
2 weeks.

· 27 ·

Green Day

One of the things I like most about the Missis-
sippi Delta in general, and my hometown of Greenville specifically, is that it has always had a cosmopolitan mix of cultures
and nationalities. When the city was incorporated after the
Civil War (during which it had been burned in the Siege of
Vicksburg), the first elected mayor was Jewish, as were the
owners of the first businesses to open. Since 1900, the majority
of the citizenry have been African American, but there is also a
sizeable Syrian population, as well as large numbers of Chinese
and Southern Italians. What we have never had in any number
significant enough to mention are Irish Americans.

This fact did not stop my mother (who, like the rest of my
family, is predominantly English) from throwing me a St. Patrick's Day party when I was in the second grade. She hung
beribboned construction paper shamrocks from the dining-
room chandelier, commissioned a sheet cake with green and
white icing from Mrs. McGraw's Bakery, and made cucumber sandwiches on rounds of white bread with homemade

mayonnaise. There's a picture of me drinking punch made of lime sherbet and ginger ale, and I remember being quietly pleased that I had the kind of mother who would throw what was surely the only St. Patrick's Day party in town. It was also the last—for whatever reason, the Celtic spirit never moved her again.

More than a decade later, I acquired a far more experienced tutor in the art of St. Patrick's Day enjoyment, my Georgetown roommate, Anne Marie Elizabeth Flaherty. Anne (nicknamed "Flaradise" by my youngest brother, who is still much taken with her paradisical charms) grew up in Boston, a city where almost 20 percent of the citizenry still refer to themselves as Irish and where close to a million people turn out for the city's St. Pat's celebration (which has included dying the Charles River green). Anne has a sister named Kerry and a brother named Danny and is so devoted to the patron saint of her home country that she imports the customs of his feast day wherever she goes.

The first time I witnessed this in action was during spring break of our sophomore year, when she accompanied me home to Greenville. Given the aforementioned population breakdown, she clearly needed to arrive well armed and she did. Not only did she pack an entirely green wardrobe, she brought an extra-large bottle of green food coloring, a useful prop that enabled her to dye every draft beer in every bar we visited. The more beer we dyed, the more popular we became, and that particular St. Pat's Day still lives on in the memory of many a townsperson.

Since then, I've made numerous trips to Anne's mother country, where I learned to appreciate the slightly more sophisticated pleasures of Black Velvets and Irish whiskey, preferably consumed in the exquisitely proportioned No. 27 Bar in Dublin's Shelbourne Hotel. A stunning view of St. Stephen's Green is afforded through the enormous Georgian windows and a perfect lunch can be had in the form of a dozen briny West Coast oysters followed by a plate of luxurious smoked salmon. Add lamb to the mix and you have pretty much the national diet of Ireland, as well as three of my very favorite foods of all time.

As the always hilarious—and spot-on—Dave Barry once wrote, "Geographically, Ireland is a medium-sized rural island that is slowly and steadily being consumed by sheep." The answer, obviously, is to consume them instead, a habit Americans have been embarrassingly slow to embrace. We eat less than a pound of lamb per capita a year, compared with a whopping 66 pounds of beef and 51 pounds of pork. The Irish, on the other hand, eat a lot of lamb—14 pounds per person to be exact, which is the same amount consumed by the English and the Spanish.

They all know what we're missing: lamb is high in protein, iron, and B vitamins, and low in fat; unlike beef, lamb contains almost no internal marbling. Not only is the majority of the fat the "good" polyunsaturated kind, it's on the outside and easily trimmed. More important, it is delicious—and the perfect centerpiece to a St. Patrick's Day feast.

To begin, I start off with a salmon rillettes recipe from another Irish Anne, Anne Kearney, the former chef at New Orleans's much-missed Peristyle, who is now chef/owner of Rue Dumaine in her native Ohio. Anne still makes this lush blend of poached and smoked salmon, but fortunately she shared her recipe with me before she left town so I don't have to fly to Dayton to enjoy it. The lamb shoulder roast that I serve as the main course is perfect for dinner parties because you can make it ahead of time and let it sit in its sauce, which is lovely on the plate mingling with a dollop of buttery "champ." The latter is a beloved Irish dish of potatoes mashed with scallions (as well as the derivation of the phrase "as thick as champ," a description which is never meant as a compliment).

For dessert, I've traded in the green-and-white cake of my childhood party for a bread pudding with Irish whiskey sauce. Unlike Greenville, my adopted hometown of New Orleans was the site of a huge influx of Irish immigrants in the 1840s and 1850s. I live adjacent to the neighborhood still known as the Irish Channel, starting point of a raucous annual St. Patrick's Day parade that features floats and "throws" including cabbages, potatoes, green beads, and, of course "to go" cups. New Orleans is also known for its bread pudding, a dessert that can be made instantly suitable for St. Patrick's Day by enlivening the sauce with Irish whiskey (try the excellent Redbreast or Green Spot) rather than the usual bourbon or brandy. By far the most popular bread pudding in town is served at the Bon Ton Café, the recipe for which I have adapted below.

BREAD PUDDING

(*Yield: 8 to 10 servings*)

1 loaf French bread, about 5 or 6 cups (a day old and a little
   dry and hard)

4 cups whole milk

3 eggs, lightly beaten

2 cups sugar

½ teaspoon ground cinnamon

2 tablespoons brown sugar

2 tablespoons vanilla

1 cup raisins

3 tablespoons butter

Preheat oven to 350 degrees.

Cut bread into 1-inch cubes and place in a large mixing bowl.
Add milk and soak for about 10 minutes. Squeeze bread with
hands until milk is well incorporated. Mix together eggs,
sugars, cinnamon, and vanilla and add to bread mixture. Stir
well and add raisins.

Melt the butter and pour into a 9×13-inch casserole dish,
making sure to coat bottom and sides well. Add bread mixture
and bake for 45 minutes to an hour, until the top is set and the
edges start to pull away from the pan.

NOTE: The pudding is even more delicious when the raisins are soaked
for a few hours in ¼ cup of the whiskey.

IRISH WHISKEY SAUCE
(*Yield: About 1⅓ cups*)

8 tablespoons (1 stick) butter

1 cup sugar

1 egg, beaten

⅓ cup Irish whiskey

In a heavy-bottomed saucepan, melt butter and add sugar. Stir constantly until sugar is dissolved. Add egg, stirring to incorporate quickly, so that it doesn't curdle. Add whiskey and stir well.

ANNE KEARNEY'S DOUBLE SALMON RILLETTES
(*Yield: 12 appetizer servings*)

1 pound fresh salmon, with blood line removed, cut into
   2-inch cubes

Kosher salt

Freshly ground white pepper

¼ cup unsalted butter, softened

½ cup finely diced shallots

2 strips lemon peel

3 cups dry white Burgundy

Juice of 1 lemon

½ pound smoked salmon slices, cut into thin strips

1 tablespoon fresh dill, chopped

2 tablespoons fresh chives, chopped

2 tablespoons crème fraîche or sour cream, plus more for
   garnish

Salmon roe

In a small bowl, sprinkle fresh salmon with salt and white
pepper and toss. Smear the bottom of a large sauté pan with
2 tablespoons of the butter, and add shallots, lemon peel, and
wine. Add salmon, spreading it out so that it is all covered and
to ensure even cooking. Bring to a simmer over medium heat
and cook until salmon is just medium or medium-well.

Remove salmon with slotted spoon and place in mixing
bowl. Reduce cooking liquid until only ¼ cup of liquid remains.
Remove and discard lemon strips and pour liquid into bowl
with salmon. Let cool for 10 minutes. Add a splash of lemon
juice, the smoked salmon, herbs, crème fraîche, and the remaining butter. Using a rubber spatula, smear the butter onto
the sides of the bowl first; then gently work the rest of the
ingredients onto and into each other. (The poached salmon will
break down into shreds.) When well combined, taste for lemon
juice, salt, and pepper.

Place into small individual ramekins or in a lightly oiled
terrine mold. Refrigerate for at least 4 hours. Serve with slices
of a skinny French baguette that have been brushed with oil
or buttered and toasted. On top of each ramekin, or on the

plate with terrine slices, garnish with additional crème fraîche and salmon roe.

NOTE: I often serve these as canapés by spreading some rillette onto the toasts and garnishing with a bit of the salmon roe and a sprig of dill or chervil. Or I fill up a crock or pretty bowl with the rillette and surround it with the toast and smaller bowls of crème fraîche and roe. Either way, the rillette will go much further—you should have about 48 servings.

IRISH CHAMP

(*Yield: 6 servings*)

3 pounds potatoes, large russets or Yukon gold

1½ cups whole milk

4 to 8 tablespoons (½ to 1 stick) butter

1½ cups scallions, thinly sliced with some of the tender green part

Kosher salt

Freshly ground black pepper

¼ cup watercress leaves, roughly chopped (optional)

¼ cup Italian parsley leaves (optional)

Peel and quarter potatoes and boil for 10 to 15 minutes in salted water until tender when pierced (but not overcooked).

Drain and return to pan and toss for a minute to evaporate all moisture.

Meanwhile, place milk, ½ stick butter, a healthy pinch of salt, and a few grindings of pepper in a saucepan with the scallions. Bring to a boil, lower heat, and let simmer for about 5 minutes. Turn off heat and let sit for about 5 minutes more.

Mash up the potatoes with a masher or a big spoon (or put through a ricer if you want a smoother mash) and add hot milk mixture, mashing as you go. Once the mixture has the consistency you like, taste for salt and pepper. Add the remaining butter, cut up in bits, and the watercress and parsley leaves if desired.

If not serving at once, wait to mix in the final ½ stick of butter, and set the pan over almost simmering water. Covered loosely, the champ will keep for an hour or more. Stir it once in a while, adding the butter right before serving.

NOTE: I often mash a pound of steamed or boiled carrots roughly into the mix (the carrots should still be a little chunky) and adjust the milk, butter, and seasonings accordingly. It's not traditional "champ" made that way, but it's delicious and really pretty to look at.

BRAISED LAMB SHOULDER

(*Yield: About 6 servings*)

One 4- to 5-pound lamb shoulder roast, boned, rolled, and
  tied

Kosher salt

Freshly ground black pepper

2 tablespoons canola oil

2 carrots, roughly chopped

2 ribs celery, roughly chopped

1 onion, roughly chopped

12 garlic cloves, crushed with flat of a knife

4 leafy sprigs thyme

2 bay leaves

1 teaspoon whole black peppercorns

2 cups whole peeled tomatoes, roughly chopped

1 cup red wine

1½ to 2 quarts chicken stock

Chopped parsley and mint

Preheat the oven to 300 degrees. Generously season lamb on all
sides with salt and pepper.

In a large ovenproof casserole or heavy pot with a lid, heat
the oil over medium-high heat. Add the lamb and brown well

on all sides. (Tongs are really helpful for this process.) Remove from pan and set aside.

Turn down heat a bit and add carrots, celery, onion, garlic, thyme, bay leaves, and whole peppercorns to pan. Cook, stirring frequently, for about 6 to 8 minutes, until vegetables begin to brown. Add tomatoes and season with salt and pepper. Cook, stirring, for about 5 minutes. Add wine and bring to a boil. Cook for a few more minutes until the wine has almost evaporated.

Return the lamb to the pan and add enough stock to come about a third of the way up the meat. Bring the liquid to a boil, cover snugly, and place the pot in the oven. After about 15 minutes, check to make sure liquid is barely simmering. Braise for about 3 to 3½ hours, spooning sauce over the meat occasionally.

Remove the lamb from the pan and transfer to a cutting board or platter. Remove string and cover with foil to keep warm.

Strain the braising liquid through a mesh strainer into a saucepan, pressing hard with a wooden spoon to push solids through. Discard the solids remaining. Let rest for a few minutes and skim the fat that will rise to the surface. Bring liquid to a boil and let simmer for about 10 to 15 minutes until the sauce is reduced and thickened. You should have about 2 cups. Taste for salt and pepper.

Slice the lamb into thick slices (they will be almost falling apart), arrange on a serving platter, and spoon sauce over the dish. (Alternatively, you can arrange them in a baking dish and reheat when ready to serve.) Garnish the platter with chopped parsley and mint and pass any extra sauce on the side.

· 28 ·

Catching Summer

The novels of Henry James have always left me a tad cold, but he was on to something when he said, "Summer afternoon, summer afternoon; to me those have always been the two most beautiful words in the English language." When uttered, they immediately conjure images of lazy days filled with hammocks and pitchers of lemonade, dog-eared books and beat-up jigsaw puzzles, long hours on the croquet lawn or playing doubles tennis. Think Mia Farrow and Lois Chiles in *The Great Gatsby* or James Salter's *Light Years* with its "lunches on a blue checked cloth" and long shadows on grassy lawns. But that's the problem—increasingly, it is only in fiction or at the movies that one encounters summer afternoons, or at least the idealized versions of them. My own are not much different than, say, my February afternoons—they just require more air-conditioning.

Of course James was writing in the nineteenth century, long before smartphones and BlackBerries, relentless e-mails and text messages, twenty-four-hour news channels and interminable streams of useless information. Unless you are almost brutally vigilant, there is no such thing as "off" time, much less whole collections of languid hours. Recently, I attended a wedding in Cashiers, North Carolina, a place notoriously lacking in cell phone coverage. During brunch at the lovely house of some friends from New Orleans, our hostess told me that at the end of most of her days there, she could never figure out what it was exactly that she had done. When I asked how they made dates for golf or dinner or a trip to the sliding rocks with no cell phone, her husband told me they made plans well in advance by post or by landline, and people simply knew to stick to them. Typically frustrated by the lack of phone coverage when we first arrived, I was almost sick when I heard the familiar beeps signifying reentry into what passes for civilization.

Every year, I vow to carve out some nineteenth-century style—or even some 1970s style—summer afternoons, and pretty much every year I fail. There have been some moments, of course. For years, my friend McGee and I spent whole hilarious days planning beach pageants with my two nieces, complete with complicated plots and elaborate costumes. One summer, my eldest niece was a reverse Rapunzel held captive beneath the sea with hair that floated upward to aid her escape, while her younger sister played her silver lamé-finned accomplice, Minnie the mermaid. My godson Barrett was Niall the Vile Crocodile and I was a seagull with feathered wings that still hang above my bedroom window in our family's house in Seaside, Florida. Our last production was an ambitious musical, with songs written on the beach with the aid of numerous frozen margaritas and my husband-to-be, who was once lead singer in a band called The Mersey Shores. I remain amazed that he married me after we cast him as the Evil Cat-fish, a role that required him to ruin a perfectly good polo shirt by sticking it with at least a dozen large fishing hooks and to writhe menacingly—and repeatedly—on the sand.

Sadly, the house's pageant box, like the jigsaw-puzzle box and the Monopoly and the Clue and the Trivial Pursuit boxes, has been left untouched for far too long. My vow is to get them all out and have at it. I also have two enormous tote bags filled with books I keep meaning to read or reread and films I've never seen. And then of course there are pitchers to be filled, lunches and dinners to be cooked and lingered over, blender drinks to be made. I once spent a whole day out on the water deep-sea fishing with friends, and when I returned to our house around five, my mother and McGee were still in their nightgowns, working on their second blender of margaritas, having spent the day watching *Lethal Weapon I, II,* and *III.* It's not exactly Jamesian, but why not?

A million years ago I bought a postcard that features a retro black-and-white image of a couple romping on the beach overlaid with a photo of a mousetrap. Across the top, it says "Catch summer before it gets away." It's a tricky business, catching summer, carving out time that adds up to a string of lazy days. One way to do it is to make late lunches or suppers that are Gatsby-esque in their elegance but simple enough to be put together at the last minute. To that end, my go-to menu for one entire summer was grilled marinated tuna steaks served with two perfect (and perfectly complementary) salads: the egg-plant salad on page 79 and another consisting of room temperature white beans (preferably a good dried brand you've cooked yourself, which can be done way ahead of time) tossed in olive oil and crumbled gorgonzola along with a handful of chopped fresh sage and freshly ground black pepper. I use the same marinated tuna in my version of a Niçoise salad, which is not only beautiful to look at, it never fails to bring the house down. All you need with it is some grilled crusty bread, lots of cold rosé wine, and a bowl of cherries or something equally easy for dessert.

GRILLED MARINATED TUNA
WITH FRESH HERBS

(*Yield: 8 servings*)

3 pounds fresh tuna, cut into 4 equal steaks

Kosher salt and freshly ground black pepper

3 tablespoons chopped mint

3 tablespoons chopped basil

1 cup olive oil

2 tablespoons lime juice

2 tablespoons red or sherry wine vinegar

2 tablespoons minced parsley

4 medium shallots, minced

Sprinkle tuna with salt and pepper and let it marinate in 1 tablespoon each of the mint and basil and 4 tablespoons of the olive oil for at least 2 hours in the refrigerator.

Combine the remaining ¾ cup of olive oil with the rest of the ingredients to make a vinaigrette. Taste to correct the seasonings and reserve.

When ready to eat, put the steaks on a charcoal grill or in a heavy-bottomed skillet (to which you've added more olive oil) and cook for about 3 to 4 minutes on each side until it is just medium rare. Remove from heat, slice in thick slices, and nap with the vinaigrette.

NOTE: Keep in mind that this recipe is a template. You can replace the mint and/or basil with cilantro, or use thyme and oregano instead (in which case I'd use lemon juice rather than lime). Sometimes I add a little soy sauce and minced fresh ginger. Remember the key to catching summer is to be relaxed about the cooking—and even a little playful.

My Niçoise Salad

For this I'm going to give you direction regarding the components of the salad rather than exact measurements.

First, make the tuna and the vinaigrette above and cut the tuna into thick slices. Then, take a big platter and make a bed of young lettuces. In the center of the lettuces, place the sliced tuna and nap generously with its vinaigrette, drizzling any that remains onto the lettuces. Next, prepare some or all of the following components and arrange in alternating little mounds around the sides of the platter.

Components:

The smallest young new potatoes you can find: Steam or boil them, halve them and toss immediately in some dry white wine until it is absorbed. Toss again with olive oil, lemon juice, salt and black pepper, and some snipped chives.

Haricots verts: Snip off the ends and steam or boil until just tender. Toss in walnut oil with a bit of sherry wine vinegar, salt and white pepper, and some minced tarragon, summer savory, or chervil.

Roasted red, yellow, and/or orange peppers: Broil them or grill them over an open flame until charred, and steam in a paper bag for 10 minutes until skins can be easily removed. Skin and seed them, cut them into strips, and toss with a little balsamic vinegar.

Japanese eggplants: Halve them, brush each half with olive oil, stud with slivers of garlic, and sprinkle with coarse salt and chopped basil or cilantro. Run under a broiler or place cut side down on a grill for a few minutes until cooked through.

Hard-boiled quail eggs, halved (you may substitute regular hen's eggs, quartered).

Niçoise olives

Enjoy!

Index